AN ILLUSTRATED HISTORY OF
MILITARY VEHICLES

AN ILLUSTRATED HISTORY OF
MILITARY VEHICLES

100 YEARS OF CARGO TRUCKS, TROOP-CARRYING TRUCKS, WRECKERS, TANKERS, AMBULANCES, COMMUNICATIONS VEHICLES AND AMPHIBIOUS VEHICLES, WITH OVER 200 PHOTOGRAPHS

PAT WARE

southwater

This edition is published by Southwater
an imprint of Anness Publishing Ltd
Blaby Road, Wigston
Leicestershire LE18 4SE
info@anness.com

www.southwaterbooks.com
www.annesspublishing.com

Anness Publishing has a new picture agency outlet for images for publishing, promotions
or advertising. Please visit our website www.practicalpictures.com for more information.

A CIP catalogue record for this book is available from the British Library.

Publisher: Joanna Lorenz
Senior Editor: Felicity Forster
Cover Design: Nigel Partridge
Production Controller: Wendy Lawson

Produced for Anness Publishing by JSS Publishing Limited
Editor: Jasper Spencer-Smith
Designer: Nigel Pell
Editorial Assistant: Lizzie Ware
Copy Assistant: Maree Brazill
Scanning: Reaction Ltd, Poole BH12 1DJ

Previously published as part of a larger volume,
The World Encyclopedia of Military Vehicles

PUBLISHER'S NOTE
Although the information in this book is believed to be accurate and true
at the time of going to press, neither the authors nor the publisher can accept any
legal responsibility or liability for any errors or omissions that may have been made.

PAGE 1: **Humber FV1600.** PAGE 2: **IFA W50LA/A.** PAGE 3: **M606 Jeep.**
PAGE 4: **GAZ/UAZ-69 Jeep.** PAGE 5: **GMC CCKW (left) and Diamond T Model 969 medium wrecker (right).**

Contents

Introduction

In 1879, Karl Benz had been granted a patent for his first internal combustion engine, and by 1885, Benz had designed and constructed the first recognizable motorized vehicle. He was awarded a patent for its invention in January 1886. Around 25 Benz vehicles were sold between 1888 and 1893, when his first four-wheeler was introduced. During the last years of the 19th century, Benz ran the largest motor company in the world, producing 572 units in 1899.

A handful of forward-thinking military officers in Europe and North America soon began to realize that the motor vehicle offered distinct advantages over the traditional horse or mule for carrying supplies, as well as being more adaptable in the prime mover role than teams of horses or steam traction engines. Within a decade, definite military roles had started to evolve for trucks, tractors, motor cars and motorcycles and, by the beginning of World War I, Germany, Britain, France, Belgium, Canada and the USA had all started the process of mechanization of their armies.

At the end of World War I, thousands of surplus military vehicles found their way into civilian hands. There was little appetite for military spending during the 1920s and, in most countries, there was little serious development in the military truck. Germany began a process of illegal rearmament in the 1930s which included some attempts at producing a range of standardized military trucks. Britain was ill-prepared for another war and, having lost literally thousands of military vehicles during the retreat from northern France, the British motor industry spent much of the next two to three years catching up and the War Office was forced to appeal to the USA and Canada for assistance.

US truck production during World War II reached a total of more than three million vehicles, and US trucks were supplied to all of the Allies under the Lend-Lease arrangements. Even Canada managed to build close to one million trucks, and the standardized Canadian Military Pattern (CMP) vehicles also became a familiar sight in all of the theatres of the war. By contrast, Germany and Japan struggled to provide sufficient logistics vehicles to their armies and were frequently forced to use captured and impressed civilian vehicles.

By 1945, German industry was close to collapse and truck production had slowed to a trickle. Most of the trucks in the hands of the *Wehrmacht* were destroyed after VE Day, while Allied surplus vehicles were disposed of in their hundreds of thousands. The armies of the newly liberated European nations were equipped with surplus British, Canadian and American vehicles, many of which remained in service into the 1970s and '80s. In Britain and the USA new vehicles were designed and produced which reflected the harsh lessons learnt in the six-year conflict. The Soviet Union also embarked on a rearmament

BELOW: **GMC 6x6 trucks leaving the D-Day beachhead. A number of amphibious DUKWS are on the beach, having ferried supplies from ship to shore.**

LEFT: **As in World War I, mud was often the greatest enemy, and without all-wheel drive it was all too easy for vehicles to be brought to a slithering halt. This column of *Wehrmacht* vehicles includes a standardized Auto-Union Horch Kfz 21 heavy personnel carrier (extreme left), a Ford V3000S or V3000A 3-ton truck (centre left), and a Zündapp KS750 heavy motorcycle combination (foreground, centre).**

programme, modelling the first generation of post-war military vehicles on the Lend-Lease trucks that had been supplied to them since 1941.

In the West, logistical military vehicles became ever more capable and sophisticated, while the Soviet Union opted for a more basic approach that relied heavily on quantity. All-wheel drive became commonplace, as did the use of diesel engines and multi-fuel units, and the availability of more powerful engines made it possible to design heavy equipment transporters which could carry tanks weighing up to 70 or 75 tons. The crossing of water obstacles remained an obsession on both sides, and the DUKW of World War II had shown that it was possible to design reliable amphibious vehicles, while many logistical vehicles were designed to be able to wade

through deep water with the minimum of preparation. Floating bridge and ferry equipment and sophisticated vehicle-launched bridges were developed that could be carried on regular trucks by both Western and Soviet forces.

By the end of the century, military vehicles had come a long way. Today's sophisticated trucks would be scarcely recognizable to the drivers and mechanics of the primitive machines known to the opposing sides between 1914 and 1918. But, curiously, many of the roles have remained unchanged.

This book explores the diversity of cargo trucks, artillery tractors, ambulances, ammunition carriers, gun trucks, and signals and reconnaissance vehicles which have always been vital to support the fighting men in every conflict across the world since the first such vehicle appeared.

LEFT: **The Bedford MK was introduced in 1970–71 as a replacement for the RL of 1951. In 1981, the MK was replaced by the near-identical, but turbocharged MJ. This example is one of those vehicles constructed by AWD after Bedford went into administration. The trailer mounts the Rapier 2000 with an Alenia Marconi "Dagger" 3D pulse doppler-radar search system.**

Military Vehicles from 1900 to 1939

The 100-year story of the military vehicle can be divided into two periods. During the first four decades of the 20th century, military vehicles differed little from civilian types. The first trucks used on the Western Front in 1914 were basic commercial vehicles. In reality, many were simply civilian vehicles commandeered by the military. Few were equipped with four-wheel drive or even pneumatic tyres. These primitive early trucks were unreliable and easily stopped by the cratered ground of the battlefield. By the inter-war period, military mechanization began, and early improvised designs gave way to purpose-built vehicles that addressed their shortcomings and vulnerabilities, resulting in the first armoured vehicles, and also vehicles designed to fulfil a range of specialized roles.

This part of the book covers the history of military vehicles from the turn of the century to 1939, beginning with the first motorized cars, lorries and trucks that enabled a reduction in the amount of horse transport used. It explains the importance of horsepower and the emergence of standardized designs, and looks at a variety of vehicles, from ambulances and artillery tractors to tank transporters and recovery vehicles.

LEFT: **A parade in Madrid, May 12, 1939, by a mechanized FlaK unit of the *Legion Kondor* (Condor Legion) in Krupp light trucks. The salute is being taken by General Franco.**

The importance of horsepower

One of the problems facing any army is the logistics of supply. The successful delivery of men and materials to the right place at the right time has frequently been crucial to the success of a military campaign. In 218BC, the Carthaginian general Hannibal used horses and elephants to move supplies from Spain to northern Italy for his 40,000-strong army. It is also said that he oversaw the construction of special barges to cross the River Rhône. Nearer our own time, Cromwell clearly understood the importance of logistics, and appointed officers to oversee transport and supplies. The Duke of Marlborough even contracted civilians to transport men and equipment for his armies and to ensure that sufficient food was always available.

Until the end of the 19th century, transport was generally carried out using pack animals and wagons. Horses, mules and oxen could be put into harness to pull a wagon, or loaded with

ABOVE: **Austro-Hungarian Army horse-drawn artillery column photographed at Galizien/Bukowina on the Eastern Front in 1915. Horse-drawn artillery was commonplace throughout the conflict.**

supplies in panniers. It was not long before the general-service type of wagon was joined by purpose-designed vehicles; for example, special wagons or carriers began to appear which could carry 24 men together with their personal equipment and weapons, and purpose-built gun carriages allowed teams of horses to pull heavy field guns. Outside of Europe and North America, camels and elephants were also used by the military.

BELOW: **Bulgarian artillery unit photographed during the Mittelmächte Offensive in October–November 1915. Each unit is drawn by four horses pulling an ammunition limber and a gun. The gun crew ride on the limber.**

This is how military transport continued until the late 19th century when a different kind of horsepower began to be developed. The Frenchman Joseph Cugnot had designed a three-wheeled steam-powered artillery tractor as far back as 1769, but it was not adopted. It was to be another 100 years before steam power began to have any significant impact on military transportation.

Towards the middle of the 19th century, the steam traction engine had started to make an impact on agricultural practice across Europe. Clearly these new machines were capable of hauling considerable loads, albeit slowly, and it was equally clear that the machines might thus have some military application. In Britain, steam tractors were used experimentally to haul heavy guns, but weight and the lack of manoeuvrability was generally a hindrance to general usage. Lighter tractors, such as the "Steam Sapper" produced by Aveling & Porter, saw service in the Boer War. The French company Lotz produced a steam-powered artillery tractor in 1867 and a number of British-built Fowler steam engines were supplied to the German Imperial Army in 1905.

By the end of the 19th century it had become obvious that mechanized transport was no passing trend and that there were real advantages to be gained from the use of motorized ambulances, wagons and staff cars. The British War Office established a Mechanical Transport Committee to investigate and report on the relative merits of steam and internal-combustion engines and to recommend suitable vehicles for military use. At first, there were doubts about the safety of petrol and the reliability of supplies, but the British Army had

purchased its first petrol-engined military vehicle in 1902, and had established a Motor Transport Company at Woolwich in 1903. By 1910 the end was in sight for steam power with the petrol engine being universally adopted as the way of the future.

In 1911, the British Secretary of War announced that he was considering the large-scale replacement of horses by motor vehicles. A so-called "subsidy scheme" encouraged civilians to purchase suitable 30cwt and 3-ton trucks at a reduced price on the understanding that they could be taken into military service should the need arise. Elsewhere, in France, Germany and in the Austro-Hungarian empire, similar schemes were established.

It was as much the availability of these trucks, as well as the appearance of the tank, which led to World War I being described as "the mechanized war".

Motor transport before World War I

In 1899, the German Imperial Army purchased its first internal-combustion engine vehicle in the form of a Daimler six-seater car. Within three years, the British Army had taken delivery of a Wolseley four-seater light car which was trialled for possible use as a staff car. In 1904, Austria had also started to buy motor cars for military use. In the USA, the US Army Signal Corps started to buy Winton cars in 1904 and, as a stand-by measure, also took delivery of some White steamers in 1910. Motorized ambulances were in use with the armies of Britain, France and the USA by 1905, often based on civilian motor car chassis.

As regards the transportation of cargo and other supplies, although the horse continued to reign supreme, the German Imperial Army had started to use Daimler Canstatt light trucks from 1900, with a medium-weight variant around 1910. Daimler had already been supplying heavy motor trucks to the Russian Imperial Army since 1903 and later to the German Imperial Army in 1907. In Britain, Leyland and Milnes-Daimler 3- to 5-ton trucks were taken into service from 1907. In the USA, trucks started to enter military service from around 1904/05, although some Woods Electric battery-powered delivery vans and cars had been purchased by the Signal Corps as early as 1899.

These early vehicles were frequently under-powered and often unreliable, but the technology was constantly improving and the military authorities in Britain and elsewhere began to organize automotive trials, which allowed the motor-vehicle manufacturers to demonstrate advances in performance. The trials often tested the products of one manufacturer against another and also allowed units of the military services to see, at first hand, how the vehicles performed.

ABOVE: **Generally only heavy steam tractors had sufficient power to move the heaviest guns. This Holt caterpillar tractor is towing a 6in howitzer.**
RIGHT: **Pre-war vehicles were frequently requisitioned by the British Army. This motor lorry, previously owned by the Anglo American Oil Company is being unloaded at Rouen, France, in 1914.**

ABOVE: **A convoy of Indian sappers travelling the dirt road towards Rufiji in German East Africa. The solid-tyred trucks are almost certainly pre-war in origin.**
LEFT: **The British Army frequently used pre-war London buses to move troops up to the front line but this early bus has been converted to a pigeon loft.**

At the same time, the motor vehicle was providing the basis for a number of specialized applications which would not previously have been a practical proposition. For example, the US Army had started to experiment with motorized scout cars before the end of the 19th century and had started to mount guns on to motor car chassis in the first decade of the new century. In France, CGT Charron had developed an armoured car as early as 1902. The same thinking led to the use of a Panhard 24CV chassis as the basis for a machine-gun car in 1906. An anti-aircraft gun had been mounted on the chassis of a De Dion Bouton 35CV car in 1910, with a similar chassis converted to carry the ammunition. Self-propelled searchlight vehicles began to appear in 1905, generally using a dynamo driven by the vehicle's engine.

By 1914, when World War I broke out, the motor truck was a well-established component of the armies of Europe's leading nations. This enabled a serious reduction in the amount of horse transport used.

The British Expeditionary Force (BEF) went to France in 1914 with large numbers of motor lorries, either of the "subsidy" type or impressed civilian vehicles, forming a well-established, functioning logistics organization. In France, large numbers of vehicles were requisitioned, while Belgium started to purchase vehicles from France, Italy, Britain and the USA. On the other side, Austria had been mechanizing its army since 1898 and was an early user of all-wheel drive designs, particularly as field artillery tractors. In Germany, something like three-quarters of the 64,000 motor vehicles available in the country in 1914 were passed into the control of the military authorities.

While it might be an exaggeration to say that there were huge advances in motor-vehicle technology during World War I, it would certainly be true to note that there were significant improvements in reliability. The motor truck of 1918 was a very different vehicle from its pre-war predecessor.

RIGHT: **The Hallford was typical of early British Army trucks used in World War I. This 1914 model was powered by a 5,300cc four-cylinder petrol engine and had a four-speed gearbox with chain drive to the rear wheels.**

Military vehicles during World War I

Although World War I was by no means the end of the use of the horse in military service, it was certainly a time when the motorized military vehicle started to develop. In fact mechanization advanced at a faster rate during this period than many would have believed possible.

The vast majority of those motor vehicles which entered service during World War I were equipped as "General Service" or cargo vehicles, and were used to deliver men and supplies to the front line, or as close to the front line as the cratered ground and primitive suspension systems would allow. However, it was not long before strategists and logistics specialist began to realize that these motor vehicles could be adapted for other, more specialized roles, including some which required the fitting of guns and crude armour. By the end of the war, there really was a surprising variety of roles for which motor trucks had been adapted, including fuel and water tankers, gun tractor, machinery workshop, artillery and ordnance repair. Other adaptions included photographic processing, gas supply, machine-gun, gun carriage, gun portee, troop carrier, searchlight carrier, signals, balloon winch, timber carrier, field kitchen, and road building vehicles.

Personnel carriers were in general not developed or required, but then World War I was not a mobile war. Nevertheless, the British Army famously used AEC Type B buses as personnel carriers in 1914–15, and France constructed personnel carriers on a De Dion Bouton and Schneider bus chassis.

As regards the technology, it must be remembered that these were early days in the development of the motor vehicle and, although a design consensus had yet to emerge, it was a period of steady development rather than of great leaps of innovation. Throughout the war, the typical engine was a big, slow-revving four-cylinder unit, generally with the cylinders cast in pairs. The valves were fitted alongside the cylinders in the block. Nevertheless, there were also examples of six-cylinder engines, and some manufacturers had already started to use overhead valves. Daimler, at least, continued to use sleeve valves.

TOP: **A US Army field radio station during World War I, circa 1917.** ABOVE: **German *Kraftfahrttruppen* mechanics working on a Praga truck. Note the chains fitted on the rear wheels designed to improve traction.** BELOW: **British-built Napier 3-ton War Office-pattern lorries awaiting delivery.**

LEFT: **A Halley 3-ton motor lorry displayed in France after being declared the winning vehicle in a reliability trial. This was based on the length of time on active service and the number of repairs required during that period.**

Most trucks had a three- or four-speed crash gearbox with final drive to the wheels by either an open roller chain or a propeller shaft. With the exception of the Austrian-built Austro-Daimler artillery tractors, two French manufacturers and the US-built Jeffery and FWD trucks, rear-wheel drive was standard. In Italy, Fiat adopted an unusual axle arrangement which employed two large T-shaped pressings for the rear axle, the rearmost pressing providing a housing for the crown wheel and pinion (differential gears). The forward pressing, which acted as a torque tube and contained the propeller shaft, was hinged to a chassis cross-member. Although pneumatic tyres had been introduced in 1887, the technology was still in its infancy, particularly for heavy vehicles; the tyres tended to be easily damaged. For this reason, trucks either retained solid tyres or had solid tyres at the rear and pneumatic tyres at the front. Brakes were almost exclusively fitted on the rear wheels or the transmission and, of course, were mechanically operated. Vehicle suspension remained primitive. Almost universally, trucks were fitted with axles mounted on semi-elliptical multi-leaf springs. Notable exceptions include the German company Büssing which fitted shock-damping auxiliary coil springs at each end of the semi-elliptical front springs.

The German companies Benz-Bräuer, Daimler and Nacke-Aquilon all produced experimental half-track vehicles during the war years. The Benz-Bräuer allowed the caterpillar tracks to be lifted and the vehicle to revert to wheeled operation.

Trailers were widely used by the German and Austrian armies. In the USA and Britain, the Knox and Lacre companies, respectively, produced tractor/semi-trailer units although, of course, they were yet to be described as such.

BELOW: **A Russian motor convoy using French Berliet trucks during World War I.**

LEFT: **Photographed on the Franco-Belgian front in 1914, these British soldiers and supplies are travelling up to the battlefront in impressed civilian vehicles.**

The World War I motor lorry

In the years leading up to World War I, the governments of Britain, France, Germany, Austria and France had all recognized the growing importance of motor trucks to the military, and had devised subsidy schemes which encouraged civilian truck users to purchase standardized, or at least unified, designs at a discounted price. In exchange for this financial assistance, the purchaser had to agree that the vehicles could be taken into military service should the need arise. Obviously such a need did arise and, from the outset of World War I, all five of these nations were in a position to supply their armies with large numbers of cargo-carrying vehicles all produced to something approaching a standard design.

In Britain, the subsidy scheme had described two classes of vehicle and, by 1913, around 1,000 of these were in civilian use. Neither class included all-wheel drive. The "Subsidy A" vehicle was rated at 3 tons, and manufacturers of such machines included Karrier, Thornycroft, Leyland, Maudslay, Rover, Dennis and Wolseley. The lighter "Subsidy B" truck was rated at 30cwt, and manufacturers of this type included Napier, Albion and Wolseley. Non-subsidy trucks were supplied in large numbers by AEC, Austin, Lacre, British Berna, Commer and Halley; the most numerous was probably the 3-ton AEC Y-Type. At the end of the war, Britain had a total of 66,352 motor trucks in service as well as 1,293 steam wagons. Thousands were put up for sale as surplus, creating a considerable problem for the domestic motor industry.

The French scheme appears to have been rather loosely defined, but purchasers of approved trucks received a subsidy of 8,200 francs in return for making the trucks available to the government for a period of four years.

LEFT: **British Army transport at La Ferte-Sous-Jouarre, using a commandeered "Robertson's Golden Shred" delivery van.**

ABOVE: **World War I was the first conflict where women had become involved in the day-to-day business of warfare, either as nursing volunteers or munitions workers.**

The German subsidy scheme, which was introduced in 1908, covered a 4-ton truck which was designed to be used with a 2-ton four-wheeled trailer. By 1914, around 500 of these vehicles were available. The manufacturers included Benz, Büssing, Daimler, Durkopp and Mannesmann-Mulag. A further 12,000 German subsidy-type trucks were produced during the war. By 1918, the German Army had 25,000 trucks in service, most of which had to be destroyed at the end of the war.

Austrian subsidy trucks were generally rated at 3 tons, and were often also used in conjunction with a four-wheeled 2-ton trailer. Manufacturers of such vehicles included Austro-Fiat, Fross-Büssing, Berna-Perl, Saurer and Graf und Stift. Although the standard Austrian subsidy truck was equipped only with rear-wheel drive, out of all the European combatant countries, France and Austria appear to have understood the importance of all-wheel drive. From around 1905, various types of heavy locomotive, suitable either for use as part of a land train or as an artillery tractor, were produced by Latil and Renault in France, and Austro-Daimler in Austria, with drive to all four wheels. Ferdinand Porsche was involved in the design of a number of these vehicles. Italian lorries of the period were built almost exclusively by Fiat, with a small number from Lancia and Itala.

The USA did not enter World War I until 1917 and was thus in a position to supply vehicles to Britain and France. By 1918, the US motor industry had produced 275,000 vehicles for the military, with thousands being put up for disposal in France at the end of the war. It is also interesting to note that the US Army was not only keen on the use of all-wheel drive vehicles, using chassis coming from FWD and Jeffery, but also tried to develop, with some degree of success, a range of standardized military vehicles including the 4x4 Militor.

At the same time all of the armies found themselves desperately short of transport vehicles, and many civilian trucks, often of less suitable design, were also purchased or pressed into service, particularly during the early years of the conflict.

BELOW: **The Irish Brigade returning to camp in 3-ton Wolseley CR6 trucks after taking Guillemont, on the Somme, September 1916.**

The US Army-standardized "Liberty" designs

Alone of all of the combatants of World War I, the US Army, through the Ordnance Department, attempted to develop a range of standardized military vehicles. The programme started in 1912 with the intention of simply providing a guide for the purchase of commercial vehicles for military use. It was also considered desirable that parts should be interchangeable across vehicles produced by a range of manufacturers. Soon the Ordnance Department was trying to develop specifications for commercial $1\frac{1}{2}$- and 3-ton trucks with both 4x2 and 4x4 drive.

In 1916, the Truck Standards division of the Society of Automotive Engineers began to draw-up standard specifications for military Class A ($1\frac{1}{2}$- to 3-ton) and Class B (3- to 5-ton) trucks, with the lighter weight Class AA ($1\frac{1}{2}$-ton) added subsequently. The specifications were issued in 1917 but before the scheme could be put into proper effect, the USA declared war on Germany. In the scramble to procure sufficient vehicles that followed the declaration of war each arm of the US military service started to purchase its own trucks. In an attempt to prevent the complete collapse of the scheme, the Ordnance Department stated that only sufficient commercial trucks should be purchased to satisfy the immediate need. Nevertheless, it is said that the US Army had a total of 294 different makes of truck in service during World War I.

ABOVE: **Not all of the trucks used by the US Army during World War I were of the Standard B "Liberty" design. Other types included Packard, Riker, White, Mack and Moreland.** RIGHT: **The 3- to 5-ton US Standard B "Liberty" trucks were produced by 15 manufacturers but were simply identified by the letters "USA" cast into the radiator header tank. The steel-spoked wheels identify this as a late model.**

Work continued on the design of what were now being described as the Standard AA, Standard A and Standard B "Liberty" trucks. Standard AA trucks were prototyped by Willys-Overland, Maxwell, Federal and Reo, powered by a 4,113cc Northway four-cylinder engine. All were replaced by the GMC Model 16, but the vehicle never entered production. The Standard A was powered by a four-cylinder 5,113cc engine and was prototyped by Autocar, Denby and White but, again, never entered series production.

Of the three designs, only the Standard B – not to be confused with the FWD Model B – entered series production. The first trucks were assembled and ready for service within 10 weeks of the standardized design being approved! There were 15 manufacturers, including Bethlehem, Brockway, Diamond T, Garford, Gramm-Bernstein, Indiana, Kelly-Springfield, Packard, Pierce-Arrow, Republic, Selden, Service, Sterling, US Motor Truck and Velie. A total of 9,452 were completed, with 7,000 being shipped overseas. The largest number came from Gramm-Bernstein and Kelly, who built 1,000 each, while Packard built just five. All of the parts were interchangeable and none of the trucks carried any manufacturer identification, the radiator header tank simply carrying the legend "USA".

The Standard B was powered by a 6,965cc four-cylinder engine driving the rear wheels through a four-speed gearbox to a worm-gear rear axle. The engines were manufactured by Continental, Hinkley, Waukesha and Wisconsin. Suspension was by semi-elliptical multi-leaf springs. Solid tyres were fitted at the front and rear.

It was a strong, durable truck, indestructible, some might say, with many remaining in military service until the 1920s.

ABOVE: **The forward-control 3-ton FWD 4x4 was widely used by the US Army during World War I. In 1916, the British company Peerless built 500 for the British Army.**

Later field modifications included the use of pneumatic tyres and the addition of front mudguards (fenders), which were not fitted during assembly.

Although the design lacked four-wheel drive, there is no doubt that the Liberty truck project was an incredible effort bearing in mind the timescale and the technology available. The project was abandoned in 1918 and the US Army effectively de-activated, but the US Ordnance Corps did not give up on the concept of standardization, returning to the idea in 1928.

ABOVE: **The Peerless TC-3 was a 3-ton truck built for both the British and US armies. The cargo body was produced by coachbuilder J. G. Brill.**

ABOVE: **Peugeot ambulance of the French Red Cross. Like many French ambulances of the period, this example appears to be built on a heavy motor car chassis. The photograph is dated 1916.** LEFT: **A British Red Cross heavy ambulance. The ambulance body is the standard British type of the period and was mounted on Rover or Sunbeam chassis.**

Motorized ambulances

The total number of men wounded during the five years that World War I raged across Europe was estimated at 22 million. Although the medical evacuation procedures of the period were surprisingly sophisticated, nevertheless the sheer numbers of casualties must have kept those concerned with their treatment at full stretch.

The first step in the evacuation procedure was often nothing more than a simple stretcher carried by two men across ground that no-one could expect a wheeled vehicle of the time to negotiate. If the casualty could not be satisfactorily treated at a field dressing station, then he would be passed up the medical chain. At the next stage in this process, it may well have been that a motorcycle was involved since many of the wounded were moved on a sidecar outfit but, eventually,

most casualties would have been moved in a motorized ambulance. This type of vehicle had started to enter military service before the outbreak of World War I and offered the benefit of speedy evacuation of the wounded. Most of the combatant nations were quick to adopt a variety of such vehicles. Many were converted from heavy motor cars or taxi cabs, while others were fitted on light truck chassis. In some cases, the casualty was carried on a stretcher which was simply slung across a tubular framework which replaced the rear body. If any weather protection was available, this was likely to be little more than a tarpaulin. One particularly primitive type was the French-built Bedelia cyclecar, where the patient was carried ahead of the driver, on a stretcher which was strapped to the bathtub-shaped body.

RIGHT: **"The Prince George", an ambulance for the Belgian Field Hospital outside Buckingham Palace, January 1916. The vehicle was presented by readers and friends of The Children's Story of the War.**

RIGHT: **Renault chassis were commonly used as a basis for ambulance conversions. Easily identified by the scuttle-mounted radiator and distinctive bonnet, the vehicle also saw service in many cities as a taxi cab.**

Some casualties were more fortunate and were carried in a vehicle which was fitted with a fully enclosed, sometimes heated, body which included space for an attendant. By the latter years of the war, the British Army, at least, had devised a standard specification for a heavy ambulance which incorporated an insulated body, heating system, and a central passage between the stretchers. Sunbeam and Rover chassis were used, and both incorporated twin rear wheels in an effort to provide a smooth ride. This question of comfort was an important issue, regardless of the type of vehicle involved. For a badly injured casualty, the often primitive suspension of the period meant that the journey must have been agony. One Fiat-based ambulance offered the combination of cast-steel wheels and solid tyres! In an effort to alleviate this discomfort, the stretcher mountings were sometimes sprung to reduce the jolting and shaking to which the unfortunate casualty would otherwise have been subjected. The British Straker-Squire and Wolseley-Siddeley ambulances of around 1906–08 actually incorporated an air suspension system for the body.

The German Imperial Army operated a fleet of ambulance road trains made up of a car towing three softly sprung two-wheeled trailers. The canvas-covered bodies each had provision for two or three stretcher cases.

In the US Army, the most common chassis for the heavy ambulance was a GMC or King, of which more than 5,500 were produced. In both cases, there was provision inside an enclosed body for eight seated casualties or four stretchers. For the light ambulance, a long-wheelbase version of the Ford

Model T was widely used. More than 10,000 were ordered during the conflict, some 50 per cent of which had been delivered by 1918. The Model T was also used by the British Army and others.

Of course, ambulances were not the only medical-service vehicles used during this period. Medical supply vehicles, mobile dental surgeries and mobile first-aid posts were also developed and mounted on suitable chassis.

LEFT: **The German Imperial Army used large numbers of these light two-wheeled trailers. Often several were coupled together to form an ambulance train for transporting the wounded. The trailer was well sprung and could accommodate two or three stretchers. Photographed on the Eastern Front in 1915.**

Improvised armour

Alongside the rapid growth in the use of motor vehicles for roles such as transporting the wounded and carrying cargo and ammunition, the opposing armies of World War I started to invent new ways in which these vehicles might be used to gain military advantage. A decade or more before the appearance of the first tanks, most of the major combatants had already begun to experiment with the use of armoured steel – often little more than heavy boiler plate – to provide some protection for crews against machine-gun fire.

In 1899, Frederick R. Simms, in conjunction with Vickers Sons & Maxim Limited, had mounted a Maxim machine-gun behind an armoured shield on a quadricycle, dubbing it the "motor scout". Simms had effectively created the first armoured car and, in doing so, had also established the three elements which remain the basics of armoured-vehicle design – firepower, mobility and protection. The French-built Charron armoured car followed in 1902, and Austro-Daimler produced a turreted four- or five-seat armoured car a year later. In Germany, Opel built its first armoured car in 1906. By 1914, wheeled armoured vehicles were being produced by most of the major combatants.

In Britain, AEC, Austin, Lanchester, Sheffield-Simplex, Rolls-Royce and Wolseley all built turreted vehicles during World War I, typically armed with a 0.303in Vickers machine-gun in a rotating turret. Peugeot, Renault and Laffly, the latter using US-built White chassis, were producing similar vehicles in France. Büssing, Daimler and Erhardt were assembling such machines in Germany. The Royal Canadian Army took delivery of 20 Autocar-based machine-gun cars in 1918. Even in Belgium, a number of improvised armoured cars were produced by adapting Minerva touring motor cars.

These early vehicles were literally "armoured" cars, little more than a front-engined heavy motor car or light truck chassis on to which had been mounted a turreted box-shaped armoured body. Engines, suspension and running gear were generally unchanged from the standard vehicle, which often

ABOVE: **An early British armoured vehicle, almost certainly improvised using a motor car chassis. There is no turret (the vehicle is clearly open-topped) but attempts have been made to protect the vulnerable radiator and the rear wheels.**

meant that the vehicle was underpowered and unstable. The increased weight also meant that the steering was heavy and the suspension prone to collapse. Most lacked all-wheel drive which meant that off-road use was also extremely limited. Whenever roads became impassable, the armoured cars could no longer be used.

The armour of these early machines was thin and generally offered protection only from small arms and rifle fire. The art of manufacturing thin armour plates was still in its infancy, resulting in wide variations in quality. Furthermore, the method of manufacture, which invariably involved bolting or riveting the plates together to form the box-like hull,

LEFT: **French Fusiliers in an improvised armoured car, crossing the Yser Canal on a locally built raft; note the hinged ramps at the rear.** BELOW: **A German car with improvised armour captured by the Belgian Army at Antwerp. In this instance, the bodywork has been left intact but has been protected by appliqué armour.**

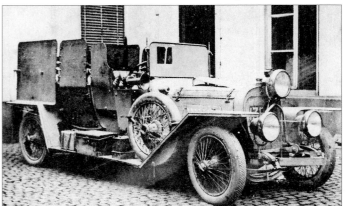

LEFT: **French Renault armoured trucks which have been fitted with a machine-gun to be used as a basic armoured car. The armoured screen, to protect the driver, would in reality give very little defence against even rifle fire.**

offered little protection against large-calibre weapons. Indeed, rivets or bolts would frequently fly out under the effect of direct hits, ricocheting around the interior and causing considerable risk to the crew. This could result in the effective loss of an armoured vehicle even though the vehicle itself remained driveable.

Armour-piercing ammunition was soon developed for rifles and machine-guns, and it was not long before this was followed by small-bore (up to 0.5in) anti-tank rifles. Even where bullets failed to penetrate the armour, the crew were still subject to the hazards of "bullet splash", where molten lead, which resulted

from the impact of a projectile on the armour plate, found its way through gaps, burning exposed skin and damaging eyes.

However, by the end of the war, it was clear that there was a continuing and valuable role for the armoured car in providing fire support for infantry and cavalry, also for conducting long-range reconnaissance missions. The early improvised designs had already given way to purpose-built vehicles that addressed the early shortcomings and vulnerabilities. Although many of these were still recognizably derived from the motor car, the design path of the armoured vehicle had already begun to diverge from standard soft-skin military vehicle design.

LEFT: **Not an armoured car but an early (1914) example of a gun portee. The weapon is a Krupps anti-aircraft gun mounted on a Daimler chassis. The elaborate curved chocks for the gun's wheeled carriage suggest that it could have been fired from this vehicle after being raised to a suitable elevation.**

The inter-war period

At the end of World War I, it was obvious that the motorized military vehicle was here to stay. Nevertheless, the demobilization of the Allied armies meant that thousands of surplus military vehicles were put up for sale to civilians. This offered many returning soldiers the opportunity to establish a transport business using a fleet of war-surplus trucks. Surplus trucks also created serious problems for the vehicle industry, which had worked hard to expand production capacity and was now faced with an unprecedented drop in demand. On the other hand, the Treaty of Versailles forced the German and Austro-Hungarian armies to hand vehicles over to the Allies for destruction. For many years, the Treaty prevented these nations from rearming.

However, even following destruction and disposal, so many thousands of vehicles remained available after 1918 that military procurement during the 1920s was at a very low level. In France, for example, some World War I vehicles remained in service right up to the outbreak of World War II. The US Quartermaster Corps had purchased fewer than 800 new vehicles by June 1929, and most of these were motor cars. Although there was little interest in rearmament in Britain, in 1923 the government had introduced a new subsidy scheme

TOP: **New vehicles outside the Marmon-Herrington factory in Indianapolis circa 1933. These 2¹/₂-ton TL29-6 6x6 trucks were designed for use as artillery prime movers.** ABOVE: **A 5-ton diesel-engined Armstrong-Saurer tested by the British Mechanisation Experimental Establishment in 1935. Saurer was a Swiss company and the truck was assembled under licence by Armstrong-Whitworth.**

for 30cwt and 3-ton vehicles, with vehicles coming from AEC, Guy, Leyland, Crossley, Morris-Commercial and Thornycroft. By 1926, some 1,000 had been acquired and registered with the authorities, but the scheme became discredited and had been abandoned by the mid-1930s.

By this time, the military organizations of most nations had virtually agreed on the categorization of cargo trucks into three classes – light, medium and heavy – even if they were unable to agree on the exact weight range for each class. But this was also a period of development and innovation, with the use of four-wheel drive becoming more commonplace. Experiments were also made with features such as four-wheel steering, lockable differentials and independent front suspension. In Britain, the War Department favoured the 6x4 format for cross-country trucks and a standardized articulated rear bogie was developed and patented by Herbert Niblett. Any manufacturer was free to use the patented design on vehicles designed to the requirements of the War Office.

Steam power was little used by any army after the end of World War I, and petrol remained the favoured fuel for the next

LEFT: **A Marmon-Herrington TH310-A6 of 1933, assigned to the US Army 19th Ordnance Company, fitted with an unusual van body.**

LEFT: **Not a manufacturer usually associated with the military, Trojan built this 6x4 truck which was trialled by the British War Office. Like most Trojans of the period it was powered by a four-cylinder two-stroke engine that the manufacturer boasted had just seven moving parts. Note the chains carried on the side step which could be fitted around the tyres of the rear bogie.**

30 to 40 years. However, the diesel engine had supporters, particularly in Germany, where Daimler-Benz, Büssing and MAN started producing military diesels from the mid-1930s.

Heavy recovery vehicles and tank transporters had yet to make any real impact. The artillery tractor was to provide the automotive designer with the greatest scope for ingenuity. French tractors from Laffly, Hotchkiss and Latil included un-ditching rollers at the front and incorporated multi-wheel steering and complex independent suspension. In Italy, the Pavesi P4-100 tractor steered on all four wheels via a centre articulated coupling.

There were also experiments with half-tracks. The first really successful half-tracked vehicles were produced in France by Citroën, using the endless rubber tracks devised by Adolphe Kégresse. The British Army tested similar vehicles from manufacturers such as Burford, Guy and Crossley using both Kégresse and Roadless track systems, but the army never made any serious commitment to the design. In the USA, the Kégresse system was adopted and modified by the US Army for the White and International half-tracks of World War II. Only Germany deployed any significant numbers of soft-skin half-tracked vehicles. These started to appear in the mid-1930s and used a more complex steel track system, with overlapping wheels and torsion bar suspension.

It was not until the mid-1930s, when Germany and Italy embarked on major rearmament programmes, that military mechanization once again started in earnest. But, by the time World War II broke out in 1939, it would be fair to say that Britain and the USA were still a long way behind in vehicle development and production.

LEFT: **First built in 1915, but remaining in production until 1920, the Fiat 20B *Autocarro-Trattore Pesante* heavy artillery motor tractor. Rather like the Trojan (above), tracks for the solid-tyred rear wheels were carried in racks on the body sides. Note the larger diameter rear wheels which were driven by chains.**

25

ABOVE: **Dating from around 1936–37, Horch, BMW, Hanomag and Stoewer produced standardized chassis for both light and medium motor cars.**
LEFT: **The US Army's 3- to 5-ton Class B "Liberty" truck of World War I was a standardized design produced by 15 manufacturers.**

The emergence of standardized designs

During World War I little attention was paid to the question of the standardization of makes, models or types of vehicle procured for military service. Nowhere was this more apparent than in the US Army, where there were reputed to be some 200 different makes of vehicle in service. The result was a logistics nightmare as supply officers and quartermasters struggled to purchase and store the parts required to maintain their mixed fleets in battle-ready condition. It is not difficult to understand why standardization might have seemed something unachievable, but during the 1920s, Italy, Germany and the USA all made some progress in this direction. For some other nations, including Britain, it was a step too far and any standardization that did take place merely allocated disparate vehicles to standard weight classes.

Despite being on the losing side during the conflict, Italy had been fortunate in one respect by virtue of having only a small number of domestic vehicle manufacturers. This had made it possible to standardize on a small number of vehicle

designs following a common layout and, in the mid-1930s, the Italian Army drew up specifications for standardized vehicles in the medium and heavy weight classes. Described as *Autocarro Unificato Medio* and *Autocarro Unificato Pesante*, the trucks were designed to carry a payload of 2½–3 tons and 6 tons, respectively. Examples were manufactured by Alfa Romeo, Bianchi, Breda, Isotta Fraschini and Lancia.

Germany was a different matter, with many competing manufacturers. In 1926, the German *Reichswehr* attempted to specify a series of standardized military vehicles, which included light (*leichte*), medium (*mittlere*) and heavy (*schwere*) personnel carriers, and a chassis for a light (1½-ton) load carrier. Within 10 years, there were so many other makes and models in service that a rationalization plan had to be drawn up. This resulted in new specifications for light, medium and heavy cars/personnel carriers and also light, medium and heavy trucks. Unfortunately, there was little real standardization achieved because manufacturers were free to interpret the requirements, including

RIGHT: **As part of the inter-war standardization programme, the 5-ton Class C truck was assembled at the US Quartermasters Depot at Fort Holabird, Maryland, for the US Marine Corps. The date is 1924.**

LEFT: **As part of the *Autocarro Unificato* programme, the Italian Army standardized trucks in medium (*medio*) and heavy (*pesante*) classes. Produced between 1940 and 1944, the 6-ton Alfa Romeo 800RE fell into the heavy class.**

the fitting of their own engines. The only truly standardized military truck produced as a result of this programme was the 2½-ton 6x6 cross-country load carrier described as the *leichter geländegängig Einheits Lastkraftwagen*. Production of the vehicle started in 1937 and continued until 1940, with examples built by Borgward, Büssing-NAG, Daimler-Benz, FAUN, Henschel, Magirus and MAN.

The US Army had enjoyed some success at standardization with the "Liberty" Standard B trucks that had been deployed during World War I but, with the war over, the design was not developed further. In the late 1920s, engineers at Fort Holabird, in Maryland, started to design prototypes of purpose-made military vehicles in a number of weight categories from 1¼ to 12 tons, with 4x2, 4x4, 6x4 and 6x6 drive. The vehicles were categorized into groups from I to V according to payload and were described as the QMC Standard Fleet. Approximately 60 trucks were completed at Fort Holabird in the early 1930s,

with the cost said to be considerably lower than that of a comparable commercially produced vehicle. It should be no surprise that political lobbying by the US truck manufacturers soon brought the programme to an end.

In the event, it seems that the dream of a truly unified range of military vehicles, sharing common parts, and equally suitable to being produced by more than one manufacturer, was one that could not be realized within technology of the 1930s. While few would have argued with the objective, it appears that the political and financial will to achieve the objective was lacking.

It would take the impetus of the coming war to bring the question of standardization back to the forefront. But it was to be Canada, rather than one of the more highly industrialized nations such as Britain, Germany and the USA, who would show the way forward with the Canadian Military Pattern (CMP) vehicles built between 1940 and 1945.

LEFT: **With almost identical vehicles produced in several load classes by both Chevrolet and Ford, the Canadian Military Pattern (CMP) trucks were probably the most successful attempt at military standardization during World War II. The smallest vehicles in the series were the 8cwt C8 and F8 trucks, which used a slightly narrower version of the standard CMP cab.**

German rearmament and the standardized military vehicle

The Treaty of Versailles, signed in June 1919, ended the state of war between Germany and the Allied powers. The Treaty required that Germany and its allies accept responsibility for having caused the war, make substantial territorial concessions, and pay reparations to certain of the Allied countries. At the same time, Germany was specifically banned from producing, manufacturing, importing, or exporting weapons, including poison gas, tanks, military aircraft and artillery. However, the Treaty was soon being undermined in small ways and, by the mid-1930s, was being openly ignored by the Nazi regime.

Rearmament in Germany started under a cloak of secrecy in the 1920s and for this reason, trucks purchased for military service were of a lightly modified civilian pattern. However, there

ABOVE: **Despite making several serious attempts to standardize military vehicle designs, the *Wehrmacht* continued to use a multiplicity of both domestic and commercial trucks.**

were problems inherent in using civilian vehicles and, by 1926, the Army (*Reichswehr*) encouraged the German motor industry to produce a series of standardized vehicles for military service. Specifications were drawn up for light (*leichte*), medium (*mittlere*) and heavy (*schwere*) personnel carriers, and a 1½-ton 6x4 chassis which would be suitable for use as a light load carrier.

MIDDLE: **Produced between 1934 and 1936, the BMW 315 was typical of German light motor cars, which used a basic civilian chassis on to which was fitted a military-type body. The chassis was also fitted with the standardized Kfz 2 body.** RIGHT: **Replacing hybrid military/civilian vehicles such as the BMW 315, the Stoewer R200 *Spezial* was a standardized light military motor car which remained in production from 1936 to 1943. Early examples had selectable four-wheel steering.**

ABOVE: **Although it never entered series production, the Trippel SG6/38 was an early attempt by the** *Wehrmacht* **to produce a practical military amphibian. The first prototypes date from 1935.** RIGHT: **For most of World War II, the** *Wehrmacht* **lacked sufficient supplies of logistics trucks and always suffered from having too many differing types in service.**

The latter went into production in 1929, firstly with Mercedes-Benz, and subsequently with Büssing-NAG, and Magirus. By 1938, some 6,000 examples had been produced. But this design was not suitable for all military uses and by 1929, it was being acknowledged that it would be necessary to design special types of motor vehicle for transporting anti-aircraft guns and field artillery. This policy led to the development of the family of standardized tactical half-track vehicles, which remained in service throughout World War II.

In 1936, the German government announced the implementation of an economic Four Year Plan which was designed to promote the development of key heavy industries, and to encourage increased domestic production of strategic materials such as steel, rubber and petroleum. By this time, there were 36 domestic motor manufacturers producing military vehicles, or vehicles which could be used by the military should the need arise. Once again, this led to a multiplicity of types being available to the *Reichswehr*. In an attempt to rationalize the situation, plans were drawn up for a series of standardized (*Einheitsfahrgestell*) vehicle chassis.

The scheme described light, medium and heavy cars/personnel carriers, and light, medium and heavy trucks. Most were fitted with an open cargo body, but different types of standardized body were also available for specific roles. All of these vehicles were to be fitted with all-wheel drive and two, three or four independently sprung driven axles according to weight classification. However, the specifications did not include any detailed aspects of design and the manufacturers were free to interpret the requirements in their own way including the use of their own engines.

In truth, the level of standardization actually achieved was minimal and the only truly standardized military truck produced as a result of this programme was a 2.5-tonne 6x6 cross-country load carrier. Described as the *leichter geländegängig Einheits Lastkraftwagen* (abbreviated to leglELkw – standardized cross-country light truck), the vehicle was effectively a product of the Ordnance Department.

Production of what was often referred to as the *Einheitsdiesel* began in 1937 and continued until 1940. Seven manufacturers, Borgward, Büssing-NAG, Daimler-Benz, FAUN, Henschel, Magirus (as Klockner-Humboldt-Deutz after 1937), and MAN were involved in production. Medium and heavy standardized vehicles were also planned along similar lines, but there never was any series production.

Unsurprisingly, the problems of a multiplicity of chassis types persisted. In 1938, as part of the Four Year Plan, General Major Adolph von Schell, Director of Automotive Affairs, once again, attempted to rationalize the number of military vehicle types in service with the intention of speeding production, reducing cost and simplifying parts inventories. Schell's office continued to oversee automobile production with regard to military requirements until it was absorbed into Albert Speer's Ministry for Armaments and War Production.

Even so, the problem was never really solved, and the *Wehrmacht* continued to struggle throughout World War II with an inventory that included too many types of logistical support vehicles.

ABOVE: **The Deutz-powered 40-ton Faun ZR was one of the few wheeled heavy tractors available to the** *Wehrmacht*.

The US QMC "Standard Fleet"

In 1918, responsibility for the design of military vehicles for the US Army had been centralized in the Motor Vehicle Board. The Board standardized three types of motor car, three motorcycles and a number of different truck chassis. By 1920, this responsibility had been passed to the US Quartermaster Corps (US QMC), but significant numbers of World War I vintage vehicles remained on strength, and purchases of new vehicles were at a minimum. Nevertheless, the QMC remained interested in standardization. In the early 1920s, the US QMC Depot at Fort Holabird, Maryland started to assemble experimental military vehicles using parts from existing types, together with production proprietary components.

By the end of the decade, the engineers involved had discovered that they were able to produce vehicles which would meet the requirements of the Army, but which would cost considerably less than the equivalent commercial product, should such a product actually be available. For the fiscal year 1930–31, the US Congress finally allocated a total of $406,800 for the purchase of new military trucks, specifiying how much could be spent on each. It proved impossible to buy vehicles of the specified performance for the stated price so the Quartermaster General proposed that the USQ MC purchase components and assemble the trucks.

A team of Army engineers led by Colonel Arthur W. Herrington who later founded the Marmon-Herrington company with Walter C. Marmon in 1931, started to build prototypes for what was being referred to as the QMC "Standard Fleet" or as USA/QMC trucks. The vehicles were classified into five groups by payload: Group I covered the weight classes 1½ to 2½ tons; Group II was for 3- to 4-ton vehicles; Group III covered the 5- to 7-ton class; vehicles in

RIGHT: **Designated TTSW (truck, tractor, six wheeled), this Hinckley-engineered 1½-ton QMC "Standard Fleet" Group I truck is fitted with twin wheels all round.**
BELOW: **Largest of the QMC "Standard Fleet" was this 10- to 12-ton Group V Sterling-engined 6x6 at Fort Holabird, Maryland in 1932.**

LEFT: **Dating from 1932, the 5-ton 4x2 Group III truck of the US QMC "Standard Fleet" was powered by a 8,210cc Hercules RXB six-cylinder engine. Compared to most vehicles in the "fleet", this appears to have been on a long-wheelbase chassis.**

Group IV had the weight range 7½ to 9 tons; and Group V vehicles were designed for a payload of 10 to 12 tons. In total, the scheme designated 129 different vehicles.

These were purpose-built trucks, assembled from carefully selected proprietary components that offered adequate power, speed and performance for the anticipated usage. Engines were supplied by Franklin, Continental, Hercules and Sterling. The smallest being a Franklin 4,490cc air-cooled four-cylinder and the largest being 12,765cc Sterling LT6 six-cylinder. Four-, six- and even eight-speed transmission was used, sometimes in combination with a two- or three-speed transfer box. Suppliers included Brown-Lipe, Wisconsin and Spicer. Axles were supplied by Wisconsin, Timken, Rockwell and Hendrickson, and the smaller trucks were generally of 4x2, 4x4 or 6x4 configuration, but in Groups III, IV and V there were also 6x6 vehicles. Suspension was by semi-elliptical multi-leaf springs.

Some 60 prototypes were built during 1931–32, and put through extensive trials both at Aberdeen Proving Ground and at Holabird, where, by all accounts, the vehicles performed well. So well, in fact, that the US motor industry felt sufficiently threatened to lobby Congress to bring the programme to a premature end. There was no series production of any of the "Standard Fleet" but the US truck industry was at least forced into producing all-wheel drive trucks that were suitable for the military. When Marmon-Herrington started producing military trucks in the 3½- to 7-ton class, the vehicles bore a remarkable similarity to some of the prototypes that Arthur Herrington had overseen for the US QMC.

BELOW: **The QMC "Standard Fleet" Group III also included 4x4 and 6x4 chassis all rated for a 5-ton payload. This is the six-wheel drive variant, photographed at US QMC Depot, Fort Holabird, Maryland in 1932.**

RIGHT: **The 15cwt 4x2 truck was one of the types most widely used by the British Army during World War II, with vehicles being produced by most of the leading manufacturers. This convoy is led by a Bedford MW, followed by a Morris-Commercial (second row, right) and a Guy (second row, left).**

British military vehicles between the wars

In 1918, after the Armistice was signed, the British Army held a stock of 165,128 military vehicles, made up of 48,175 motorcycles, 43,187 motor cars and ambulances, 66,352 trucks, 1,293 steam wagons, and a further 6,121 miscellaneous vehicles. Thousands were left in Europe, but hundreds more were parked in vehicle dumps in Great Britian, and the Government started to dispose of these surplus vehicles through a series of auctions starting in the spring of 1919.

The Army kept sufficient for immediate requirements, but so many trucks remained in service that there was little need to purchase any new vehicles for most of the 1920s and thus equally little need for development. One exception was the series

of abortive experiments with full- and half-tracked trucks that had been carried out under the aegis of the Department of Tank Design and Experiment at Woolwich. By 1923, these trials had been abandoned as impractical and expensive. There were later experiments with half-tracked vehicles using the Citroën-Kégresse and Roadless systems, but the British Army did not procure any significant numbers.

However, there remained a shortage of medium-weight vehicles and in 1922 a new subsidy scheme was introduced which covered 30cwt and 3-ton vehicles. There was little interest from the motor industry until the following year when some aspects of the specifications were simplified.

ABOVE: **The 15cwt Commer "Beetle" of 1939 was never produced in significant numbers.** LEFT: **Although the design was patented, the WD standardized rear bogie was used by several manufacturers producing 6x4 trucks for the British Army. Thornycroft elected to use their own double-sprung bogie.**

Albion, Karrier, Clement-Talbot and Crossley all built prototypes. In 1925, Guy, Halley, Thornycroft and Vulcan also built prototype vehicles. A plan to extend the scheme to cover 15cwt vehicles was abandoned.

In 1924, Louis Renault had produced a 6x4 heavy motor car which he believed could offer similar performance to the rival Citroën-Kégresse in cross-country performance. One of these was acquired by the Royal Army Service Corps (RASC) Training College. The rear wheels of the Renault were mounted on two axles in a self-contained bogie which was articulated to the frame in a way that allowed maximum ground contact regardless of the terrain. Realizing the advantages of this, but believing that the design could be improved, Colonel Herbert Niblett and his team designed and patented an improved version which was known as the "War Department Pattern articulated rear bogie". The bogie was suitable for both 30cwt and 3-ton vehicles and could be used freely by any manufacturer designing vehicles to meet the requirements of the British Army. By 1927, most of the big manufacturers in the British truck industry were producing subsidy vehicles, but the specification was not updated again and the design soon became obsolete.

It was also at this time that responsibility for the research, experimental work and design of British military vehicles was transferred from the Department of the Quartermaster General to the Master General of Ordnance. The RASC resisted the change, arguing that valuable experience would be lost, but it was to no avail and the Mechanical Warfare Experimental Establishment (MWEE) was created to oversee the function.

The MWEE established a series of annual vehicle trials in which manufacturers could demonstrate their trucks against those of competitors in the hope of being rewarded with valuable military contracts. These trials were held from the mid-1930s on the mountain roads in north Wales and were intended to encourage technological development. All types of experimental vehicles were tested, including a number from overseas

ABOVE: **The 3-ton 6x4 Leyland Retriever was typical of British heavy military trucks in service during the late 1930s.**

manufacturers. It was all a curiously gentlemanly business and the British truck industry appeared as reluctant to try new ideas as the Army was to buy them.

By the time the Government realized that another war with Germany was inevitable, it was suggested that the answer to the shortage of general transport vehicles lay in being able to impress or hire suitable civilian trucks. By 1938, the RASC had compiled a register of 10,000 vehicles which could be readily mobilized should it become necessary. It would be true to say that few, if any, of these were really suitable, but did at least allow the existing military 6x4s to be replaced in the general service role and converted for more specialized tasks.

So, when the British Expeditionary Force left for France it was equipped with a miscellany of some 85,000–100,000 often ageing and unsuitable vehicles. Most were abandoned in May 1940, and many foolishly believed that this presented the perfect opportunity for future British military vehicles to be manufactured to a standardized design.

LEFT: **Soldiers of the 1st Battalion of the King's Own Scottish Borderers prepare their Morris-Commercial 6x4 vehicles in Nazareth, November 17, 1936.**

Artillery tractors, tank transporters and recovery vehicles

During World War I the largest vehicles used by the opposing sides were those deployed for moving heavy artillery. Often steam powered, and almost universally heavy and slow, these vehicles continued to develop through the post-war years. But, as artillery pieces became more sophisticated, the weight and size for a given calibre were reduced, allowing the tractors to become more manageable in size. The typical artillery heavy tractor of the 1930s was a steel-bodied truck, which provided accommodation for the gun crew together with supplies, equipment and ammunition. The artillery piece was mounted on a wheeled carriage. A powered winch was almost always provided to assist with emplacing and recovering the gun.

Tanks were another matter altogether and the trend over the years was for tanks to become ever larger and heavier. At one end of the scale, the French Renault light tank of World War I weighed little more than 7 tons. Although no trucks of the period were capable of carrying such a load, by 1921, Charles Dewald of Paris had demonstrated a 7¹/₂-ton truck that could carry the tank on the flat bed, loaded by means of a capstan winch. The vehicle was copied by other nations who found that the smaller tanks of the period could be accommodated relatively easily as trucks became more powerful. The US Army used a development of the Mack Bulldog with a special flat-bed body for this purpose. There was even a tank carrier of this type in the US QMC "Standard Fleet". In the mid-1930s, the French

ABOVE: **The Scammell Pioneer 6x4 chassis was developed in 1929. It was ultimately used as a tank transporter, heavy artillery tractor and recovery vehicle by the British Army.**

Army developed a flat-bed tank carrier which used an overhead hoist for loading. Both Britain and Germany continued to use flat-bed tank carriers into the early years of World War II, but the heavy tanks presented a different problem.

During World War I, the typical British heavy tank weighed some 28 tons. This was way beyond the capacity of the trucks of the period and tanks were either moved under their own power or were loaded on to flat-bed railcars. In 1919, the London-based company H. C. Bauly modified an AEC K Type truck by mounting a fifth-wheel coupling across the rear axle. This allowed a semi-trailer, designed to carry a large crawler tractor or a medium tank, to be towed. The vehicle was close to being a tank transporter in the modern sense and would appear to have shown the way forward, but it was to be a further 10 years before the first specialized tank transporter appeared.

In 1929, Oliver North designed the Scammell Pioneer. A huge machine for the time and intended as a heavy tractor for pipeline work, Scammell realized that it also had military potential. In 1932, the British War Office purchased a single petrol-powered Pioneer, together with a low-loading trailer capable of carrying 18 tons. The trailer featured a removable rear bogie which allowed a tank to be easily loaded. It appears that, at first, the Army failed to see how such a vehicle might be useful and the vehicle was quickly assigned for training duties. It was not until 1937 that further purchases were made when the original was replaced by an updated version, this time with a 20-ton low-loading trailer.

The rear-mounted loading ramps, which these days provide the normal means of loading tanks on to trailers, did not appear until 1939. As a tractor-trailer configuration with a heavy-duty loading winch and hinged ramps, the Scammell Pioneer effectively became the modern tank transporter.

But it was not just the transportation of tanks that was creating problems – recovery was also an issue. Disabled tanks were frequently recovered using a heavy breakdown vehicle and a suitable drawbar trailer. The increasing weight of many trucks also demanded heavier recovery vehicles. The British Army had purchased a number of FWD R6T 6x6 tractors equipped for the heavy breakdown role in 1929, and this tractor was often used with a tank-transporter trailer. When the R6T was found to be unable to move the increasing weight of tanks and other vehicles, it was superseded by a recovery version of the same

ABOVE: **In the artillery tractor role, the Pioneer was designated R100. The spacious steel body had room for the gun crew plus supplies and ammunition. The gun is a British 60pdr on a pre-World War II solid-tyred carriage.** BELOW: **Dating from 1929, the FWD R6T was used both as a recovery vehicle (shown) and as an artillery tractor. AEC took over production in 1932.**

powerful Pioneer 6x4 chassis. It was a similar story in the USA, where the M1 6x6 heavy wrecker was originally developed as a tank transporter in the late 1930s.

Inevitably, the outbreak of World War II served simply to further increase the weight of tanks, bringing a fresh set of technical challenges.

LEFT: **Although first designed in 1928, the US Army's TCSW (tank carrier, six wheeled) eventually formed part of the US QMC "Standard Fleet". Rated at 7½ tons, and assigned to Group IV, the steel body incorporated folding ramps at the rear. The vehicle is the second prototype, dating from 1930; later vehicles were fitted with pneumatic tyres.**

Other specialized roles

The inter-war years saw the motor lorry gain universal acceptance as the primary military logistics vehicle. Although the vast majority of such vehicles were bodied for the cargo role, the inevitable advances in technology allowed adaption to other more specialized roles.

Aircraft refuelling

During World War I aircraft had generally been refuelled manually, simply by pouring fuel into the tanks from containers. But the use of ever-larger fuel tanks made it imperative to find a better way of dispensing fuel. Hand pumps on trolleys soon gave way to trucks that were fitted with a large cylindrical fuel tank. A motor-driven pump and hose apparatus were fitted to deliver the fuel to the aircraft tanks. By the outbreak of World War II, the RAF had developed three types of such vehicle using chassis built by Albion, Morris-Commercial and Karrier.

Bridging vehicles

The crossing of water obstacles has always played a part in warfare. The destruction of bridges can delay an advancing army just as surely as a shortage of men or ammunition; and

TOP: **Commer Q2 complete with the 3-ton "Queen Mary" trailer used for transporting aircraft.** ABOVE: **Sharing many components with the Model O853 Matador artillery tractor, the AEC Model O854 chassis was used as an 11,350 litre/2,500 gallon aircraft refuelling tanker. Pumping equipment was fitted in a compartment at the rear of the tank.**

all armies have sought the means to overcome such delays. The Romans used the fascine, a bundle of sticks or brushwood, to facilitate ditch crossing. The technique continued through World War I and persists today, although the brushwood has given way to plastic piping.

RIGHT: **In Britain, as in the USA and Germany, new vehicles were generally reserved for the military services. Although closely related to the military designs, the Bedford OWS tractor, complete with Scammell tanker semi-trailer, was allocated to the Petroleum Board for essential deliveries.**

LEFT: **Albion BY5 bridging trucks used by the Royal Engineers. The chassis was built to carry pontoons for building a floating bridge. A collapsible boat could also be carried.**

The first regular bridging train in the British Army was formed in 1812, using floating pontoons to form a crude ferry. While development of this technology continued, the tanks of World War I suggested that there were other ways to cross, at least, smaller water obstacles and a small portable bridge was designed by William Tritton of William Foster & Company. A Foster tractor was modified to carry Tritton's bridge, which could be positioned across a 2.5m/8ft gap in around three minutes. Other designs which emerged at the time included the sledge bridge, designed to be towed into position by a tank and the canal lock bridge which was lowered across the gap.

While these early designs required the weight and power of the tank for reliable deployment, smaller types of bridge which could be carried by a specially adapted truck began to appear in the 1930s. The British Army, for example, used several types of bridge during this period, including the prefabricated floating pontoon bridge, trestle bridge, small box girder bridge and the sliding bay bridge. All could be carried on a fleet of typical 3-ton 6x4 military trucks.

Signals and communications
Primitive mobile wireless equipment had been used during World War I and had even been truck-mounted to allow mobility. Dogs had been used as cable layers, the lightweight signals cable simply being free to unroll from a reel carried on the dog's back. During the 1920s and 1930s advances in wireless technology allowed smaller, more powerful, equipment to be vehicle-mounted. It became possible for reliable speech and Morse transmission to be made on the move. Tanks and fighting vehicles were fitted with wireless equipment that allowed the commanders to communicate, and keep in contact with mobile command posts. Cables could be laid by means of special equipment mounted on trucks or trailers. Telephone switchgear could also be vehicle-mounted.

Workshop facilities
The development of small mobile generators and relatively lightweight lathes, power drills and heat-treatment facilities allowed quite sophisticated workshops to be mounted on the chassis of a typical medium truck. This was a practice that had actually started during World War I, but the general workshops of that period soon gave way to more specialized workshops devoted, for example, to ordnance or motor vehicle repair.

ABOVE: **A Bedford MWC chassis on which has been fitted a YMCA canteen body.**

Military Vehicles from World War II to the Present Day

The advent of World War II changed everything, and the design of trucks for the military and civilian markets began to diverge. Few civilian companies had any need for all-wheel drive, or for vehicles that could float or be driven in deep water. Specialized vehicles began to emerge, including powerful artillery tractors, missile transporter-erector-launchers, tank transporters, bridging vehicles and amphibious vehicles. In the six decades since the end of World War II, this divergence has continued. Most military planners recognize that standard commercial vehicles are fit only for non-battlefront duties. The modern purpose-designed military vehicle is a powerful and manoeuvrable machine, which has little similarity to the design of vehicles available for use by commercial companies.

This part of the book focuses on the development of military vehicles in Germany, Britain, the USA, Canada, the Soviet Union and Japan, and explores post-war designs such as air-portable vehicles, reconnaissance and special operations vehicles, cargo vehicles, ambulances, communications vehicles, heavy equipment transporters, missile transporters, bridging vehicles and amphibious vehicles.

LEFT: **A line-up of restored GMCs. Note the .50in Browning heavy machine-gun on the third truck in line, typical of air-defence vehicles used on the supply routes.**

LEFT: **Canadian Military Pattern (CMP) vehicles were used by Canada, Britain and the Commonwealth countries. The standardized vehicles were produced in a range of load classes, and fitted with a wide range of bodies.**

Military vehicles during World War II

When Britain declared war on Germany in September 1939, British forces were ill-prepared and ill-equipped. The invasion of France which followed the six-month "phoney war" was ill-advised and was unlikely to succeed. Germany had been mobilizing for war since the mid-1930s, while Britain had spent little on rearmament during that period, hoping that a major conflict could be avoided. The events of May 1940 were a serious setback and, at the time, it appeared that there was little prospect of help from the USA who believed that this time Europe should sort out its own problems.

Few would have dared to predict the long struggle that lay ahead. World War II became a truly global conflict and there is little doubt that the pressures and exigencies of the moment created an incredible technological hothouse effect which, among other things, had an enormous influence on the design of military vehicles. Certainly for Britain and the USA there was little comparison between the vehicles that were in service at the beginning of the conflict and those being produced in 1945.

ABOVE: **The GAZ-67 was the Soviet equivalent of the US Army's Jeep.**

It was not a contest of equals and each of the participating nations brought its own particular strengths and weaknesses to the battlefront. The British Army had been forced to abandon thousands of military vehicles in France in 1940. Faced, then, with terrible shortages of all kinds of equipment Britain took whatever was available from the domestic motor industry, with little standardization between the products of different manufacturers. The result was that many vehicles were far from satisfactory and the Army faced an ongoing logistical nightmare in producing and distributing parts to keep this fleet of vehicles running.

The situation in the USA was an altogether different matter. When the USA finally realized that the war in Europe really was a global affair, that nation's massive industrial production capacity rightly earned it the title of the "Arsenal of Democracy". The USA was more successful in standardizing on a small number of specialized military vehicles, concentrating on turning these out in large numbers for all of the Allies. The standardized Jeep, GMC, Chevrolet, and Dodge vehicles played a valuable part in the conflict, but there were also trucks from many lesser known companies, including Available, Hug, Biederman, Thew, Hendrickson, Walter, Sterling and Corbitt.

Canada understood the significance of standardization, but perhaps with just three domestic manufacturers this should be no surprise. The standardized Canadian Military Pattern (CMP) vehicles combined technical competence with ease of production and might be considered to have established a pattern for the design of military vehicles in the post-war years.

Curiously, Germany was behind in innovation, producing military vehicles which were technically superior, but were complex and difficult to produce in sufficient numbers. It is a paradox that the nation that invented the concept of Blitzkrieg entered the war at least partially dependent on horse-drawn transport, mounted troops and a multiplicity of civilian vehicles.

LEFT: **Fiat's TM40 4x4 medium artillery tractor. Also available with solid tyres, it was powered by a 9,365cc six-cylinder engine. It was also built as a truck (T40) with an** *Einheits* **cab.** BELOW: **The British-built Ford WOA1 was based on the company's pre-war Model 62 and produced from 1941 to 1947. The example shown is a staff car, but there was also a heavy utility vehicle (WOA2) built on the same chassis.**

Rearmament had started in earnest with Hitler's rise to power in 1933, and military spending rose accordingly. Truck manufacturers were encouraged to produce any vehicle thought to be worthy. By the middle of the decade, there was such a multiplicity of vehicle types in service that several attempts were made to reduce the number of designs, to little avail.

Germany entered the war with far too many different types of vehicle and with an obsession with technical quality that slowed production. There was also a heavy reliance on civilian and captured vehicles that exacerbated the problem. As the war progressed, Allied bombing began seriously to affect the ability of the German motor industry to produce sufficient transport vehicles. Many vehicle types were simplified, while others were abandoned in an attempt to maintain production – but it was probably too late to affect the outcome of the war.

In the end it was down to volume – standardization did not win the war, but standardization and simplification allowed production to be maintained at the highest levels.

LEFT: **Produced from 1941, in two wheelbase lengths and with both open and closed cabs, the GMC CCKW 2¹/₂-ton 6x6 truck was used by all of the Allies in every theatre of the war. A total of more than half a million were built. The truck was to become the logistics "backbone" of many countries around the world after the end of the war.**

Changing technology and the importance of all-wheel drive

Although Germany had embarked on a programme of rearmament during the mid-1930s, little attention was paid to the question of logistics. Like most of the major combatants of World War II, Germany entered the war with vehicle designs that dated from the first half of the 1930s. Clearly the design of motor vehicles had rapidly progressed since the first faltering military applications during World War I. Outside of Germany, there had been little progress in the design of purpose-built military vehicles; the majority of the vehicles in use during the 1930s were recognizably derived from civilian designs.

However, there were two major areas of diversion between military and civilian vehicle technology – the first was in the provision of all-wheel drive, the other was in the use of all-wheel steering.

All-wheel drive

During World War I, driven front axles had employed simple Hardy-Spicer universal joints and, although these were fine for use at limited speed, it was not until the invention of the constant-velocity (or homo-kinetic) joint that the modern all-wheel drive vehicle became a possibility. The constant-velocity joint allows a smooth transfer of power to the wheels regardless of the angle to which the joint is bent. The first such joint was patented by Pierre Fenaille in 1926 under the name Tracta and was promoted by the French designer Jean-Albert Grégoire in his front-wheel drive motor cars.

ABOVE: **Most nations tested four-wheel steering during the late 1930s but eventually rejected the idea as dangerous. This is a Mercedes-Benz G4.**

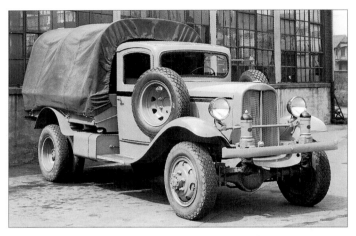

ABOVE: **The Marmon-Herrington company was one of the pioneers of four-wheel drive in the USA, supplying conversion kits to other manufacturers as well as building trucks to their own designs.**

A year later, Alfred H. Rzeppa produced the joint vehicles which bore his name – it was a better product but was expensive to manufacture and maintain. This was followed by the more cost-effective Bendix-Weiss joint.

RIGHT: **In the 1930s, the British War Office appeared reluctant to accept that all-wheel drive had any real benefits. It was believed that 6x4 trucks fitted with a WD-pattern standardized rear bogie could provide almost the same level of performance. Here a Thornycroft 6x6 is undergoing trials.**

LEFT: **The crew of this 30cwt Canadian Chevrolet 4x2 of the Long Range Desert Group (LRDG) are using sand channels in an attempt to extricate the vehicle from soft sand. Stripped-down Chevrolets were typical of the type favoured by the LRDG for operations in Egypt in 1940. The steel rear body was a Gotfredson design of all-welded construction.**

Despite the ready availability of these joints, the use of all-wheel drive for military vehicles was by no means universal in 1939. While Germany had developed a range of all-wheel drive light car and truck chassis, in Britain, for example, the War Office had placed greater emphasis on the use of the 3-ton 6x4 chassis. Britain had produced all-wheel drive artillery tractors, but the only 4x4 trucks were prototypes produced in very small numbers by Guy and Karrier for trials in 1938.

The advantages of all-wheel drive soon became obvious, and, as the war progressed, Britain, the USA and Canada began to produce more all-wheel drive vehicles. By 1945, there is little doubt that, for military trucks, such vehicles had become the norm.

Four-wheel steering

While all-wheel drive became more commonplace as the war continued, the early experiments in the provision of all-wheel steering were quickly abandoned.

The German standardized light car chassis (*leichter Personnenkraftwagen* or I Pkw) of 1936 was produced with both four-wheel drive and selectable four-wheel steering. It must be presumed that the use of four-wheel steering was intended to enhance manoeuvrability. The Willys Jeep, which followed in 1940, was also prototyped with steering on both the front and rear axles.

The complexity of the linkages involved and the general unpredictability of handling when all-wheel steer was selected soon led to the abandonment of the technology.

Diesel engines

There was one other major area of development where it could be argued that military vehicles lagged behind contemporary commercial practice and that was in the application of diesel power. The world's first compression-ignition engine was developed by Dr Rudolph Diesel in Augsburg, Germany, between 1893 and 1897. It was not

until 1923 that compact diesel engines that were suitable for use in commercial trucks were produced by Daimler-Benz and MAN in Germany. The use of such engines became more widespread in the early 1930s in commercial vehicles, but two schools of thought seem to have emerged over the use of these more efficient power units in military trucks.

Germany and Japan were both forced to synthesize fuels, and since diesel oil was easier to produce, it is not surprising that both nations were enthusiastic users of the diesel engine. However, in Britain, Canada and the USA, despite the use of powerful diesel engines in tanks, the diesel-powered military vehicle remained in a minority. Notable exceptions include the Scammell Pioneer and the Diamond T Model 980/981.

ABOVE: **A Jeep fitted with experimental wheel extensions to provide traction through deep snow (known as "Spuds" when used on tanks).**

RIGHT: **A steel-cabbed Ford V3000S bogged down in the mud of the Russian Front as a VW *Kübelwagen* struggles past. Small numbers of the V3000S were also produced with all-wheel drive.**

German military vehicles

Despite explicit prohibitive conditions laid down in the Treaty of Versailles, during the 1930s Germany had embarked on an ambitious illegal programme of rearmament, spending millions of *Reichmarks* on tanks, armoured vehicles, U boats, artillery and aircraft and other military equipment. The number of men serving in the German Army increased ten-fold and the army was re-equipped and trained in the lightning Blitzkrieg tactics. However, it appears that little attention was paid to the design and procurement of the logistics vehicles that were required to support this formidable war machine.

Perfunctory attempts had been made at standardizing trucks during the mid-1930s, but the numbers of different types of

motor vehicle in use were still spiralling out of control. Over a period of years, two separate attempts were made to rationalize the types of vehicle and, for much of the war, the military struggled to maintain hundreds of different vehicle types.

In 1938, Major General Adolph von Schell, Director of Automotive Affairs, attempted to reduce the number of military vehicle types in service with the intention of speeding production, reducing cost and simplifying parts inventories. According to records of the *Fahrzeugministerium* (Motor Vehicle Ministry), the number of truck types, which had previously totalled 131, was reduced to 23. The number of car types was reduced from 55 to 29. Manufacturers in the occupied countries were also enlisted

ABOVE: **A Mercedes-Benz ambulance Type L1500S which served with the 12th SS Panzer Division *Hitlerjugend*.** RIGHT: **Early examples of the Stoewer R200 *Spezial* light car were fitted with a four-wheel steering system. The chassis was also produced by BMW and Hanomag. Most were fitted with a four-seat passenger car body, but other variants included a signals car, maintenance/repair vehicle and light survey car.**

into producing trucks to German designs, but the Army was not averse to using impressed civilian vehicles – French-built Citroën and Renault trucks were widely used – or to purchasing the products of the Czechoslovak companies Tatra and Škoda. None of this helped with vehicle standardization.

Three years later, the number of cars was reduced further, with only the Volkswagen *Kübelwagen* remaining in production. At the same time, production of the previous, often complex, *Einheits*-pattern vehicles was terminated and all future German military trucks were standardized in four weight classes – $1^1/_2$, 3, $4^1/_2$ and $6^1/_2$ tons, each of which included both S *Typ* (4x2, standard) and A *Typ* (4x4, *Allradantrieb* – all-wheel drive) variants. At the same time, von Schell rationalized the 164 types of dynamo, 269 light bulbs, 113 starter motors and 112 hydraulic cylinders that the army was forced to stock in order to keep the trucks serviceable.

Although existing vehicles remained in service, including many pre-1935 *Reichswehr* types, which were frequently of civilian pattern, no more were built. The trucks of the von Schell programme were of simplified design and were easier to manufacture. In some cases, more than one manufacturer was contracted to produce the same type of vehicle. But the problems continued and, in October 1943, more vehicle types fell victim to the standardization programme and, by the end of the year, there were just nine different types of truck being produced. Light trucks were produced only by Steyr and Phänomen; medium trucks came from Opel, Daimler-Benz (who were producing the Opel design under licence), Ford and Borgward. Heavy trucks came from Daimler-Benz, Büssing-NAG, and Tatra, the latter, a decidedly non-standard 6x6 design with a V12 air-cooled diesel engine. Continued shortages of materials also led to the adoption of the *Wehrmacht Einheitsfahrerhaus* cab of compressed

ABOVE: **Although it lacked all-wheel drive, the VW *Typ* 82 *Kübelwagen* was the *Wehrmacht*'s closest equivalent to the Jeep. Some 52,000 were produced.**

cardboard and timber that could be fitted to any of the standardized vehicles of the von Schell programme.

After this date, there was also a marked preference for diesel engines, since the fuel was easier to produce. By mid-1944, Magirus diesel engines were being used in trucks produced by other manufacturers.

Even if the problems of standardization had been solved, there were also continual difficulties with procurement and Allied bombing. This combined with a lack of production capacity, meant that there was a continual shortage of vehicles. During the period 1939–45, the USA manufactured more than three million soft-skin motor vehicles, Britain produced 680,000 and Canada delivered more than 810,000. By contrast, the German motor industry believed that world domination was possible with less than 500,000 transport vehicles.

LEFT: **The *Wehrmacht* was always an enthusiastic user of *Halbkettenfahrzeug* (half-tracked vehicles). Dating from 1934–35, the Krauss-Maffei-m-8 medium artillery tractor was also built by Daimler-Benz and Büssing-NAG. Early examples had shorter tracks with four road wheels. The vehicle is towing a 15cm sFH 18 howitzer.**

45

British military vehicles

Britain had failed to recognize the threat posed by the rapid rearmament of Germany, initiated in 1936, and had not spent sufficient time or resources in re-equipping its own armed forces. Many prototypes had been designed and tested during the closing years of the decade, but few had

TOP: **Dating from the immediate pre-war years, the 15cwt Bedford MW remained in production until 1945, with some 66,000 completed.**
ABOVE: **The light utility vehicles – known as "Tillies" – were produced by Hillman (shown), Austin, Morris and Standard.**

been cleared for production. When Britain declared war on Germany in September 1939, the British Army was equipped with a miscellany of motor vehicles, many of which were obsolete. Almost all of the British vehicles in service in 1939 lacked front-wheel drive and the most numerous types were the 4x2 15cwt, as typified by the Bedford MW and the Morris-Commercial CS8. The 30cwt and 3-ton 4x2 and 6x4 trucks were typically produced by Morris-Commercial, Leyland and Thornycroft dating from the early 1930s.

Just 5,000 of the vehicles shipped to France with the British Expeditionary Force (BEF) in 1939 were returned following the rescue from Dunkirk. Faced with a devastating shortage of vehicles, and the threat of imminent German invasion, the Government had little choice. All civilian motor vehicle production was halted and the motor industry was put on to a war footing. There was little time available to develop new designs, which meant that many pre-war types were continued in production. Many of the vehicles which remained in production for the duration of the conflict were far from satisfactory, but possessed the sole virtue of being available. At the same time, Britain turned to the USA and Canada for assistance, resulting in an enormous variety of vehicle types in service.

There was little co-operation between manufacturers and no standardization of even the most basic design elements. Consider the "Tilly", a British light utility vehicle which, during the early days of the war, served in many of the roles for which the Jeep was so well suited. Little more than a pick-up truck based on a 10hp or 12hp motor car, the "Tilly" was produced by Austin, Morris, Hillman and Standard. Each vehicle was produced to its own design and lacked all-wheel drive. No attempt was made to encourage the four manufacturers to standardize design.

At the other end of the scale, the Scammell Pioneer chassis was used as a heavy tractor for tank transport, a heavy recovery vehicle and artillery tractor. It was slow, but possessed a sturdy reliability which endeared the vehicle to its crews but, for the entire duration of the war, was in short supply. In the tank-transporter role, the Pioneer was supplemented by the superb US-built Diamond T, and by the somewhat less-than successful Albion CX24S, which possessed brakes so inadequate that drivers were obliged to use the engine and transmission to reduce speed, leading to many crankshaft breakages. However, the shortage of heavy artillery tractors meant that the British Army was obliged to operate the diesel-engined Scammell alongside the similarly equipped Albion CX22S and the petrol-engined US-built Mack NO series.

British all-wheel drive trucks started to be produced in 1940, but were never available in sufficient numbers to replace the 4x2 and 6x4 types. Dating from February 1941,

LEFT: **Morris-Commercial C8 field artillery tractor. A typical load for these tractors was the British 17 or 25pdr field gun on a two-wheeled carriage, together with a two-wheeled ammunition limber.**

Bedford's forward-control 3-ton QL was probably the most successful. Other 3-ton trucks were produced by Albion, Austin, Thornycroft, Karrier, Fordson, Guy and Crossley, with no attempts made to standardize design or components.

By VE Day, the British Army possessed 1¼ million logistics vehicles, but resources were wasted through abortive attempts to produce British versions of standard US-designed vehicles. Austin and Standard, for example, were asked to investigate the production of a British Jeep. Austin prototyped a substitute for the ¾-ton Dodge WC series. Thornycroft designed an eight-wheel skid-steer amphibian which could have replaced the DUKW, but the production vehicles, assembled by Morris-Commercial, did not perform to specification, mainly due to inadequate development at prototype stage. Like Germany, Britain struggled through World War II trying to produce and support too many makes and types of vehicle.

ABOVE: **The 3-ton WOT6 was Ford's largest World War II military vehicle, with more than 30,000 produced from 1942–45. Most were fitted with the standard cargo body, but there were also breakdown, container and machinery variants. The truck was fitted with a V8 side-valve petrol engine.**

ABOVE: **The Scammell Pioneer R100 was the British Army's largest artillery tractor. Although lacking front-wheel drive, the slogging power of the Gardner 6LW diesel engine gave the vehicle superb haulage capacity. Approximately 780 examples were built between 1939 and 1945.**

US military vehicles and Lend-Lease

In September 1939, the British Army had in service 85,000 motor vehicles, slightly less than one-third of which were impressed civilian types. At the end of May 1940, the British Expeditionary Force (BEF) was forced to abandon thousands of military vehicles in France following the retreat from Dunkirk. Most were destroyed, but many were painted grey by the Germans and given a new lease of life. Faced with a desperate shortage of all types of vehicle, Britain turned to the domestic motor industry for assistance and, at the same time, appealed to the USA and Canada. US-built vehicles, which had been destined for France, and may have been paid for by France, were diverted to Britain. At the same time, the British Government started placing orders with truck manufacturers in the USA to help bolster the inadequate supplies coming from the British factories.

ABOVE: **GMC CCKW (left) and Diamond T Model 969 medium wrecker (right), both fitted with the canvas-topped military cab adopted to reduce steel consumption and to provide a reduced shipping height.**

When Britain declared war on Germany in 1939, the US Government had changed its neutrality law to allow the nations that were at war in Europe to buy military vehicles and supplies from the US. During most of 1940, Britain was obliged to pay for those vehicles which came from the US, including tanks. It soon became obvious that Britain, standing alone against the might of Hitler's Germany, was facing a serious financial crisis.

British Treasury officials convinced President Roosevelt and Treasury Secretary Henry Morgenthau that, if Britain were to continue to hold back the German war machine, then some form of credit or loan would be required. In the face of US public opposition, Roosevelt was anxious that the USA should not be drawn into another European conflict. At the same time it must

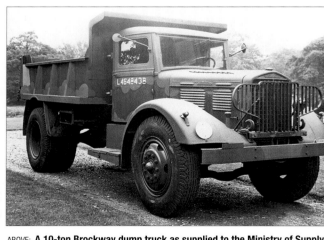

ABOVE: **A 10-ton Brockway dump truck as supplied to the Ministry of Supply during early World War II.** LEFT: **Dodge 1½-ton WC62 weapons carrier.**

ABOVE: **The Diamond T Model 980/981 was produced in both open and closed cab form and was initially intended for the British. It was adopted by the US Army as the M19 tank transporter initially classified as "substitute standard", later downgraded to "limited standard" when the M26 "Dragon Wagon" entered service.**

ABOVE: **Rated at a nominal 7½ tons, the Mack NO was a heavy prime mover intended for towing the US Army's 8-inch howitzer or the 155mm field gun.**

have been obvious that the survival of Britain was in the best interests of the USA. By December 1940, Roosevelt thought of a way of providing aid to Britain that did not involve the use of the words "loan", "credit" or "subsidy". On March 11, 1941, US Congress passed the "Lend-Lease Act" into law, enabling the mighty industrial base of the USA to produce and supply hundreds of thousands of tons of military equipment to America's wartime allies without leaving a residue of war debts when the conflict was over.

Lend-Lease continued until the end of the war and the USA supplied somewhere around $42 billion in food, military goods, oil and fuel, industrial production and technical services. More than $2 billion, some 4.9 per cent of the total aid, was in the form of motor vehicles and parts, with a further $3.5 billion (8.4 per cent) in the form of tanks and armoured fighting vehicles. Britain and the Commonwealth were the major beneficiaries of the scheme.

Lend-Lease goods were also delivered to China and the Soviet Union. Lend-Lease ensured that American tanks, Jeeps and trucks became a familiar sight wherever the Allies were fighting.

Well-versed in mass-production techniques and safe from German bombing raids, for six years the US automotive industry turned out millions of rugged, reliable trucks and the parts to keep them running. In 1945, these vehicles would go on to provide the backbone of the armies of the newly liberated European nations, as well as providing the pattern for military vehicles produced the world over during the next two decades.

There is little doubt that by agreeing to become the "Arsenal of Democracy" the USA ensured that Germany could not win World War II. Aided by the English Channel and Hitler's ill-advised invasion of the Soviet Union, Britain had managed to hold out against Nazi Germany. There is no doubt that Britain or the Soviet Union would not have been able to defeat Germany without the industrial and military might of the USA.

LEFT: **Using the same cab as the more numerous GMC CCKW and powered by the same six-cylinder engine, Chevrolet's 4100/7100 series was produced in a range of variants, including this earth auger (drill) intended for erecting telephone poles. Production began in 1940 and continued to the end of the war.**

RIGHT: **January 1, 1941, two US soldiers in a ¹/₄-ton 4x4 Willys MA Jeep prior to the entry of the United States into World War II.**

The Jeep

In June 1940, William F. Beasley, Chief Engineer of the US Ordnance Department, produced a small sketch for an open-sided four-wheeled all-wheel drive utility vehicle that was intended to replace the motorcycle and the horse and rider in the military reconnaissance role. Some preliminary work had been carried out in conjunction with American Bantam that had helped to refine the specification of what was wanted, but, in mid-July, 135 motor manufacturers in the USA were approached to bid for the detailed development and eventual production of the vehicles. Just two companies responded – American Bantam, who believed that they were already ahead, and Willys-Overland.

Having appointed Karl Probst to head the design team, American Bantam had their bid papers approved within the allotted 10-day period and had a prototype running by late September. Given the opportunity to examine the Bantam prototype, the Willys-Overland vehicle was delivered some eight weeks later, on November 13. Political pressure was put on the Ford Motor Company and their prototype was submitted 10 days later. All three of the companies involved had experienced difficulties in achieving the Ordnance Department's target weight, but the Jeep was still light enough to be man-handled when necessary. Inside the simple open bodywork there was room for four men, and there was a mounting for a machine-gun or anti-tank rifle. This vehicle was also equipped to tow a

field gun. For the first time, the US Army had a light four-wheel drive vehicle that could go almost anywhere that a tracked vehicle – or a motorcycle – could go.

ABOVE: **Early Willys MBs had a slatted radiator grille. Note the "A" frame which allowed two Jeeps in tandem to tow a light field gun.**

Following a period of trials, the Ordnance Department was undecided as to the relative merits of the different vehicles. The three companies each received a contract to build 1,500 examples of their vehicles based on Beasley's design – the Bantam was described as the 40BRC, Willys designated their vehicle MA and the Ford was known as the GP.

Once the manufacturing work was underway, elements of the Willys and Ford vehicles were combined to produce a standardized design which was described as the Willys MB, and the Ford GPW – the "W" indicating that the Ford included elements of the Willys design. Bantam received no further contracts, but Willys and Ford went on to build some 640,000 examples of the standardized Jeep between 1941 and 1945.

The MB/GPW was light enough to be able to go almost anywhere and yet powerful enough to be able to carry out tasks that the designer had almost certainly not envisaged. Although it dated from the early 1930s, Willys' Go-Devil four-cylinder engine, which was also used in the Ford GPW, was superbly reliable. When coupled to a three-speed gearbox and two-speed transfer box, it allowed a maximum road speed of 106kph/65mph, combined with the ability to tackle the worst possible terrain.

The availability of large numbers of Jeeps brought to an end the widespread use of the military motorcycle. For example, US Army standing orders had initially decreed that motorcycles be attached to each armoured division, but this practice came to an end in March 1942 when the vehicle type was removed from the "Tables of Organization and Equipment" (TOE), having been replaced by the Jeep.

ABOVE: **The Willys MA was the improved version of the company's Quad prototype, the immediate predecessor to the standardized MB/GPW. A total of 1,500 examples were produced during 1941, most of which were supplied to the Soviet Union. The model differed from the standardized Jeep. Note the radiator and grille and the depth of the body cut-outs. A column gear-change was fitted.**

The Jeep demonstrated that it was possible to provide effective four-wheel drive for a light military truck. Vehicle types such as the British light utilities became obsolete. It was no longer necessary to compromise on transport for officers in the field, the Jeep was equally useful on or off the road. During the course of World War II, senior figures such as Churchill, De Gaulle, Patton and Montgomery – even European royalty – were all photographed riding in Jeeps.

LEFT: **Designed by the US company American Bantam and the US Ordnance Department, the Jeep was the first vehicle of the type that effectively replaced the motorcycle in military service. In the standard form some 640,000 Jeeps were produced by Ford and Willys-Overland.**

Canadian Military Pattern

ABOVE: **Chevrolet C8A; with variations, the type 1C house-type body was used for various roles, including ambulance (1C5), heavy utility (1C7), radio (1C2), machinery (1C10) and staff car (1C11).**

In 1937, Syd Swallow, an engineer with the Ford Motor Company of Canada, designed what was effectively a Canadian version of the 15cwt British War Office-pattern truck using a strengthened chassis from a Ford 1-ton commercial vehicle. The Ford prototype was followed by a similar vehicle from General Motors, Oshawa. A year later, the Canadian Army asked Ford and GM to produce a light version of the 6x4 Scammell Pioneer, which the British Army was using as a heavy artillery tractor. The resulting prototypes were displayed at Petawawa alongside a 6x6 Marmon-Herrington. From inauspicious beginnings these vehicles became a range of standardized Canadian military vehicles. At first described as "Department of National Defence Pattern" (DNDP) they were subsequently to be better known as the "Canadian Military Pattern" (CMP). The vehicles followed British War Office patterns, but were designed for mass production in Canada.

In truth, neither Ford nor General Motors believed that the essentially British design of the vehicles was suited to Canadian production methods and produced alternative specifications. But the Department of National Defence in Canada insisted that the trucks be produced according to the British pattern.

In late 1939, it was proposed that the vehicles be fully standardized and that Ford produce the cab, engine and transmission, with GM contributing chassis, axles and body. This idea was eventually dismissed and both companies went on to build their own versions. Although there was a

high degree of commonality, the Ford-built vehicles were powered by a 3,917cc V8 side-valve petrol engine driving through a four-speed gearbox; if the vehicle had all-wheel drive then a two-speed transfer box was fitted. However, General Motors vehicles used a 3,548cc six-cylinder overhead-valve petrol engine, with the same drive-line assembly. Ford fitted "split" axles, while GM fitted "banjo-type" axles.

The earliest vehicles to be supplied were of the 4x2 pattern, but 4x4, 6x4 and 6x6 vehicles were subsequently produced. The smallest CMP vehicle in the family was an 8cwt,

RIGHT: **Chevrolet CGT field artillery tractor; a similar vehicle was also produced by Ford, designated FGT. The body was based on then-current British War Office practice. The vehicle was generally used as a tractor for the 25pdr field gun and its ammunition limber.**

ABOVE: **The 30cwt CMP truck was designated C30 or F30 according to manufacturer and most were of the 4x4 configuration.**

ABOVE: **Chevrolet C15A bodied by the British company Edbro as a mount for a 20mm anti-aircraft gun.**

designated either C8 (Chevrolet) or F8 (Ford), according to manufacturer. If the chassis was fitted with all-wheel drive the designations became C8A and F8A. Next was the 15cwt chassis (C15, C15A, F8, F8A), followed by a 30cwt (C30, C30A, F30, F30A) design. Largest of the series was the 3-ton chassis, which was produced in 4x2 and 4x4 long-wheelbase (C60L, CC60L, F60L, FC60L), and in 4x4 short-wheelbase form (C60S, FC60S). There were also 3-ton 6x4 (F60H) and 6x6 (C60X) chassis, and Ford also produced a 2-ton 4x2 in both long- and short-wheelbase. The 6x4, which was only built by Ford, was unusual in that the front axle and the forward of the rear axles were driven.

Standard variants included cargo, artillery tractor, workshop, breakdown, heavy utility, machinery, ambulance, recovery, wireless, anti-aircraft, van, office, water tanker, fuel tanker, anti-tank portee and stores. There were also armoured variants. Regardless of manufacturer, the vehicles shared a common cab design, only the details of how the cab was mounted to the chassis varied. The first type of cab – described as the Number 11 – was copied from the British cabs of the period and received considerable criticism, being cramped and hot. It was soon replaced by the Number 12 cab; this was a little better, and featured an alligator-type bonnet to improve engine access. The most numerous of the designs was the Number 13 cab which was fitted from late 1941. The cab featured the distinctive reverse-slope windscreen.

The majority of the vehicles were shipped to Britain first in completely knocked down (CKD) form, and subsequently in semi-knocked down (SKD) form for local assembly. In Britain, large numbers were assembled at the Citroën works in Slough, and at Pearsons in Liverpool. There were many instances where Ford-built cabs were fitted on to GM chassis and vice-versa, because shipping losses caused an imbalance in the availability of components. In Australia,

the vehicles were assembled by Holden and were often fitted with locally produced bodies.

Less than 15,000 vehicles were produced in 1939, the first year of production, but by 1941, Canada was the largest producer of motor vehicles in the British Empire. By September 1, 1945, Canada had produced almost 410,000 CMP vehicles, of which the largest number were of the 3-ton 4x4 type. The CMP vehicle was probably the most successful example of standardization during World War II and was used by all of the Allies. Thousands remained in service in Europe after the end of the war.

ABOVE: **Chevrolet C15A 15cwt general service cargo truck. Both 4x2 and 4x4 chassis were produced. The cab is a 1941 Number 12 design with an "alligator" bonnet.**

RIGHT: **The GAZ-61 was produced between 1941 and 1948. It was effectively a 4x4 version of the GAZ-11-73. Powered by a 3,480cc six-cylinder petrol engine, it was widely used as a staff car for junior and middle-rank officers.**

Soviet military vehicles

Dating from 1924, the first Soviet-built truck was the 1½-ton AMO-F-15. The Moscow-based AMO plant was renamed ZIS in honour of Joseph I. Stalin (Zavod Imeny Stalin) in 1933. AMO and GAZ became the two most significant truck plants in the Soviet Union. The GAZ factory in Nizhni Novgorod had been constructed during 1931–32 with American assistance and was equipped with tooling for the Ford Model A shipped from the Ford plant in Germany. By 1932, GAZ was producing what were essentially Ford Model A trucks and cars under the designation GAZ-A and GAZ-AA, with a GAZ-AAA 6x4 truck variant entering the

range in 1935. During the second Five Year Plan, Soviet factories produced some 200,000 vehicles. Although the output of trucks grew at an impressive rate during the period 1933–38, the vehicles were essentially civilian in design and little attention was paid to the needs of the military.

When the Soviet Union was invaded by Germany on June 22, 1941, the Red Army was equipped with standard GAZ and ZIS trucks, the design of which dated from the beginning of the 1930s. Faced with the might of the *Wehrmacht*, it was clear that the nation's factories were not in a position to produce the modern military vehicles that would be required to mobilize

LEFT: **ZIS-5 searchlight trucks. Powered by a 5,550cc six-cylinder engine, the ZIS-5 was rated at 3 tons and produced from 1933 to 1944. The vehicle was often nicknamed the "Stalin Truck". Variants included cargo, gas producer, compressed gas carrier and dump truck.**

ABOVE: **Produced for a decade or more from 1943, and powered by a licence-built Ford engine, the GAZ-67 and 67B was the Soviet version of a Jeep-type vehicle.**

ABOVE: **The Jeep was not the only vehicle supplied to the Soviet Union under the Lend-Lease Program. Trucks were supplied from the USA, Britain and Canada. For example, Studebaker supplied more than 100,000 US6 trucks. Introduced in 1941, the US6 was produced as a 6x6 and 6x4, the latter designated US6X4. Other vehicles supplied to the Soviets included GMC CCKW trucks, Dodge T214s, GPA amphibians, Chevrolet and Dodge trucks as well as Mack tractors.**

the Red Army. But, help was soon available. In November 1941, the Soviet Union was included in the US Lend-Lease arrangements and, between 1941 and 1945, US aid to the Soviets amounted to 16.6 million tons of material at an overall cost of almost $10 billion. This included more than 400,000 trucks and tank transporters as well as artillery prime movers, guns and armoured fighting vehicles.

Alongside the US-built trucks, which included Chevrolet, Studebaker and GMC, Jeeps, Dodge and Mack vehicles were also delivered. Vehicles were also supplied by Canada and Britain. At one time, almost half of Soviet military supplies were being carried in Lend-Lease trucks. The Soviets also used large numbers of captured vehicles.

The 1½-ton GAZ-AA was replaced by the modernized GAZ-MM in 1938, although the improvement was confined to the use of a more powerful engine. Both this, and the GAZ-AAA remained in production throughout the war years but, in 1942–43, GAZ started to produce a second generation of military vehicles, based on the Lend-Lease

types which had been coming from the USA. First of these was the GAZ-64 (later GAZ-67) a small 4x4 field car similar to the Jeep. Heavier trucks were produced in small numbers by the JAG (YAG) and JAS factories. Also a number of half-tracks were produced using the ZIS-5 chassis, under the designation ZIS-33 and ZIS-42.

The German invasion forced the relocation of the ZIS plant from Moscow to the Urals where it was known as either Ural or Ural-ZIS, and later UAZ. Production was restarted in the new factory in 1943.

Many of the Lend-Lease vehicles remained in service during the immediate post-war years. It was not until almost the late 1950s that the Soviet Union began to produce modern military vehicles. The GAZ, ZIS (now renamed ZiL) and UAZ plants continued to be the major suppliers.

LEFT: **Russian anti-aircraft troops on parade in unidentified trucks with planes flying overhead in Kiev, 1935.**

RIGHT: **Japanese forces enter Peking, China, July 31, 1937. The light tank is at the head of a column of Isuzu Type 94 trucks.**

Japanese military vehicles

The world force that is today's Japanese motor industry is a comparatively recent phenomenon. At the end of the 1920s, the Japanese home market was dominated by the products of the United States "big three", General Motors, Ford and Chrysler. The domestic manufacturers had assembled less than 500 vehicles a year. In 1931, the Japanese Government purchased some 6x4 trucks from Britain and Czechoslovakia and set about developing designs using the vehicles as patterns. The Government also set up a Motor Industry Establishment Committee to produce a specification for a standardized medium truck that could be used by both civilians and the military.

The military vehicle divisions of DAT and Ishikawajima were merged to form a new company to manufacture what was effectively a subsidy-type truck. The company was named Jidosha Kogyo and the products were designated Isuzu. The first product of the new company was the Isuzu TX, a 4x2 civilian truck rated at 2 tons and powered by a 4,390cc six-cylinder engine. The larger TU10 was a 6x4 design rated for 3 tons which was also produced as a military vehicle, the Type 94 – the number being derived from the Japanese date 2594 (1934). Three years later, a 4x2 version was produced, designated Type 97.

In 1936, the Japanese Imperial Army had decreed that all Japanese vehicle manufacturers should agree to produce

RIGHT: **The Isuzu TU10, or Type 94A, was first supplied to civilians under a subsidy scheme, and rated at 3 tons. The chassis was assembled in several factories. The vehicle was one of the Japanese Imperial Army's standard tactical trucks.**

LEFT: **The 1¹/₂-ton Isuzu Type 94 appeared in 1934 and was the Japanese Imperial Army's standard cross-country truck. Based on typical European practice of the early 1930s, it featured a 6x4 drive-line and was produced in a variety of configurations. The Type 94A was powered by a petrol engine; the 94B used a diesel power unit.**

products under military licence and that 50 per cent of the capital, shareholders and company officials should be Japanese. By 1939, all production of American cars and trucks in Japan had ceased and the factories had been taken over by local companies. From 1941, military trucks were being produced by Nissan (formerly DAT), Isuzu and Toyota. During 1941–42, the three companies produced 45,500 trucks and buses, approximately half of which were intended for military use.

Following the Japanese attack on Pearl Harbor in December 1941, the motor industry was placed under direct government control and civilian output was severely restricted. Truck production was reduced by American air raids. Shortages of raw materials, and the pressures of manufacturing aircraft engines saw production continue to decline during the years that followed. Just 6,726 vehicles were produced in 1945. Continual shortages of petrol forced the Japanese to develop a family of standardized diesel engines which were intended for use in trucks, tanks and submarines.

Standard military trucks deployed by the Imperial Army during World War II included the Nissan 80 and 180, a semi-forward control 1¹/₂-ton vehicle powered by a 3,670cc six-cylinder engine; a 1¹/₂-ton Toyota, equipped with a four- or six-cylinder engine, and designated G1, GA, GB, AK, KB or KC according to date and specification; and the 1¹/₂-ton 6x4 Isuzu Type 94 and the 4x2 Type 97. Isuzu also produced 2-ton trucks in both 4x4 (designated YOK1) and 6x6 (ROK1) form, as well as a 3-ton 6x4, the TU23 of 1941, built in both petrol- and diesel-engined form. The heaviest Japanese trucks of the period were the 7-ton Isuzu Type 2, a 4x2 cargo truck powered by an 8,550cc engine, and the 20-ton Isuzu TH10 dump truck that was produced for the Japanese Imperial Navy.

Isuzu and Ikegai produced half-tracked vehicles with multiple crew seats in an open body, very much in the German style. Both were designated Type 98, indicating that the date of introduction was 2598 (1938), and were powered by a six-cylinder standardized diesel engine. The vehicles were intended for use either as artillery tractors or as mounts for anti-aircraft guns. The Army also used large numbers of captured American and British vehicles.

BELOW: **The Nissan 180 was produced from 1940 until 1944. After the war, the vehicle continued in production for the civilian market and was rated at 2¹/₂ tons. This captured example was photographed at Aberdeen Proving Ground, Maryland, USA.**

Half-tracked vehicles

During World War I, continuous heavy shelling of the front line, combined with the inevitable flooding of the shattered ground, frequently rendered huge areas all but impassable to wheeled vehicles. With their endless track systems, the early tanks and heavy artillery tractors were less easily defeated by ground conditions. However, their unreliability and the lack of suspension made for a slow and uncomfortable ride, and even a tank of the period was easily defeated by a water obstacle.

Searching for improved mobility, in 1915 the French Delahaye company had produced a tracked bogie which could be used to replace the rear wheels of a conventional vehicle. During World War I, the German Daimler company had also started experimenting with trucks on which the rear wheels were replaced by a tracked bogie and, in the USA, both Holt and Lombard had also produced primitive half-tracked machines.

The first successful vehicle of this type to be developed was almost certainly the Citroën-Kégresse half-track of the early 1920s. Adolphe Kégresse had developed his endless rubber track system to enable the Russian tsar to drive with equal facility over metalled roads, deep mud and snow in what was effectively little more than a modified car or light truck. His system demonstrated how the mobility of wheeled vehicles could be improved without necessarily involving the expense and complexity of a fully tracked machine. Forced to leave Russia after the 1917 Revolution, Kégresse brought the system back to his native France,

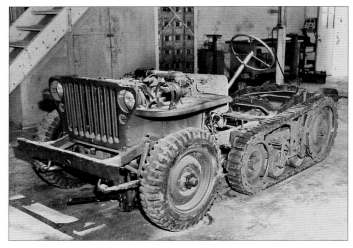

ABOVE: **Although there was no series production, there were experiments conducted in the USA with a view to producing a half-track Jeep.**

where he managed to convince André Citroën that there was merit in developing half-tracked vehicles for use in the French territories overseas, where metalled roads were poor or non-existent.

The French Army started to buy half-tracks and there were demonstrations of the system in Britain and the USA. Despite experiments with half-tracked vehicles from Albion, Burford, Guy and Crossley, the British Army remained unconvinced. In the USA, Kégresse tracks were fitted to a Model T Ford, but it was experiments by GMC, Cunningham and Marmon-Herrington with the US Ordnance Department which led to the appearance of the well-known armoured US half-tracks of World War II, using a heavily modified form of the Kégresse bogie and suspension system.

RIGHT: **Load-carrying 3-ton truck constructed using the chassis of the Sd Kfz 11 medium half-track; these vehicles were built by Hansa-Lloyd-Goliath, Borgward, Adler, Horch and Wanderer (both of them part of the Auto-Union conglomerate), Hanomag, and Škoda. The cab is typical of the utility *Einheits*-type fitted to German trucks from late 1943, while the bonnet and radiator grille do not conform to the standard pattern.**

ABOVE: **Japanese Ikegai KO-HI Type 98 semi-track prime mover. Produced from 1937 as a tractor and self-propelled mount for anti-aircraft guns.**

ABOVE: **Italian-built Fiat 727SC** *trattore semi-cingolato* **(half-tracked tractor). It was fitted with a Fiat 5,750cc six-cylinder petrol engine and a five-speed gearbox with reduction gear, giving ten forward speeds.**

There were also US experiments with a half-tracked Jeep, using at least two different track systems, and an experimental 2½-ton half-tracked truck was built by Autocar for possible use in the Soviet Union.

Half-tracked cars and trucks were also produced in the Soviet Union by both ZIS and GAZ. The vehicles were generally based on a conventional wheeled chassis, but the lack of front-wheel drive and use of low-powered engines restricted their performance.

In Germany, a series of standardized half-track vehicles was developed in six weight classes from the mid-1930s. Eschewing the endless rubber Kégresse bogie, the sophisticated German half-tracks employed pin-jointed all-steel tracks suspended on torsion bars or semi-elliptical leaf springs. The vehicles were originally intended for use as prime movers for artillery, but, late in the war, their weight, expense and complexity saw them

replaced by the *Maultier* – a standard military truck on which the rear wheels had been replaced by a far simpler track system. In Britain, the bogie system of a captured German 8-ton Sd Kfz 7 half-track was used by Bedford to produce a prototype artillery tractor dubbed the Traclat, but there was no series production and the idea was abandoned once the war was over.

After 1945, the improvements in all-wheel drive trucks saw the half-tracked vehicle fall from favour.

BELOW: **Chassis for the** *schwere Wehrmachtsschlepper* **(sWs) heavy half-track tractor. Designed by Büssing-NAG, the first prototype appeared in the spring of 1943. The vehicle's appearance was that of a heavy truck to which had been fitted a standard rear track and bogie assembly.**

RIGHT: **By the end of World War II, the US Army was experimenting with ever larger and more powerful trucks. Designated T20, this chain-driven 8-ton 8x8 cargo vehicle was produced by Cook Brothers in late 1944. The engine was a 9,865cc Continental six-cylinder producing 240bhp. The vehicle was also prototyped as a tractor-truck, but there was no series production of either type.**

The end of World War II

As World War II progressed, it was not only the military strengths and weaknesses of the opposing sides that became more apparent. Faced with relentless Allied bombing, Germany's industrial capacity was being slowly eroded, forcing the High Command to decide on military priorities. Choosing tanks and guns over transport vehicles, the German truck industry practically stopped and such development as did take place was directed towards saving scarce raw materials.

Continued shortages of materials also led to the adoption of the *Einheitsfahrerhaus* cab in October 1943. It was fabricated from compressed cardboard on a timber frame, to save vital supplies of steel, and could be fitted on any standardized truck chassis that remained in production.

In Britain, the motor industry continued to mass-produce trucks, but these were to the same designs that had been in production since the early years of the war. Precious little time was available to think about developing new designs or even of making modifications which might improve some of the existing vehicles. One notable exception was the Leyland Hippo Mk II, a 10-ton 6x4 truck that was specifically designed in 1943 to meet the needs of the military. Various experimental vehicles were produced, including the Bedford Traclat, a half-tracked light artillery tractor that borrowed heavily from German practice. Prototypes were built for Albion and AEC of low-silhouette heavy artillery tractors. Albion designed the curious double-ended 8x8 tank transporter. None entered series production.

Similarly, in the USA, the motor industry continued to produce the trucks which had helped the Allies, while the US Ordnance Department was also working on new designs. In 1941–42, there were experiments with low-profile versions of existing 3/4-ton 4x4 trucks, as well as designs for low-profile 2 1/2-ton 6x6 trucks and 3-ton 4x4s. Prototypes of these vehicles were produced by, among others, Dodge, GMC, Corbitt, Reo, International and Ford. None were put into production, but the work did lead to the development of the 1 1/2-ton 4x4 Ford GTB.

The Ordnance Department was also investigating the development of larger trucks which could provide greater mobility combined with increased load-carrying capability.

ABOVE: **The British-built Leyland Hippo Mk II was a 10-ton cargo vehicle intended for long-distance road use in Europe following the D-Day landings.**

LEFT: **The British had
not tended to use
half-track logistics
vehicles during World
War II. The Bedford-
built Traclat (Tracked
Artillery Tractor) was
prototyped towards
the end of the war.
The track system
is an obvious copy
taken from a German
heavy half-track.**

In 1942, Cook Brothers produced a strange rear-engined chain-driven 8x8 vehicle which was used for desert mobility trials in California. This went no further, but some of the drive components were re-used in prototypes for an 8-ton 8x8 cargo truck and tractor, designated T20. This was also produced by Cook Brothers in 1943–44 using a Continental six-cylinder engine in combination with a five-speed gearbox and two-speed transfer box. A similar machine was produced by Corbitt, featuring turntable steering and a swan-necked

chassis frame designed to reduce the overall height. Sterling used the same approach for the 12-ton T26 8x8 cargo truck, which was powered by a LaFrance V12 engine. The company also produced a tractor variant. Corbitt designed an 8-ton 8x8, designated T33, with a Continental engine.

The end of the war saw most existing military vehicle contracts cancelled, leaving many uncompleted. At the same time, all urgency for further development was lost. Although more than one of these huge trucks survived into the 1950s before being scrapped or otherwise disposed of, none of the designs were put into production.

ABOVE: **German truck production and development had virtually come to an
end by early 1945, but from October 1943 most trucks were fitted with the
Einheits utility cab.** RIGHT: **Singularly unsuccessful, the double-ended Albion
CX33 heavy tank transporter was an interesting development. There were
two engines, originally driving all eight axles, but later modified to 8x6.
The rear cab housed the winch controls.**

The immediate post-war years

During World War II, the USA, Britain and Canada produced approximately five million military transport vehicles. In May 1945, following VE Day, hundreds of vehicle production contracts were cancelled. In Europe there was an abundance of surplus military vehicles for which there was no longer any demand. There is a persistent story that few trucks were returned to the USA, manufacturers there being anxious to avoid a repeat of the market collapse which had followed the repatriation of surplus vehicles after Armistice Day in 1918. "War Claims Settlement" agreements were made between Britain, the USA and Canada which provided for the disposal of unclaimed vehicles and other assets remaining in Britain. Huge dumps were established across Europe where vehicles were examined – the worst vehicles were scrapped, cannibalized or simply dumped in the sea. The best were allotted for further

ABOVE: **At the end of the war, hundreds of outstanding contracts were cancelled, and surplus military vehicles were collected in large open areas to be disposed of by auction.**

military use, but the remainder were auctioned or sold to civilians as surplus. There were also thousands of tons of vehicle spares stored in depots across the world.

Thousands of surplus military vehicles were gifted or sold to the newly liberated European nations. France, Belgium, Denmark, Norway and the Netherlands all mobilized their post-war armies with a miscellany of pre-war vehicles and Allied vehicles of US, British and Canadian origin. Only France standardized on US-supplied equipment and, for a period, even new French military vehicle designs tended to follow the same basic specifications.

ABOVE: **Although thousands remained in service, surplus Jeeps were also sold to civilians and many were modified to match the owners' preferences.**
LEFT: **Much modified, the powerful Pacific M26 made an excellent heavy-haulage tractor for Wynns Heavy Haulage.**

In Britain, all military vehicle contracts came to an end. Sufficient vehicles were retained for the Army's immediate need, and the numbers and variety of types of truck in service were rationalized. Most of the vehicles retained were of British manufacture, but the bigger, more specialized US-built vehicles, such as the Diamond T and Mack tractors, were retained, as were thousands of Jeeps. Plans were put in hand for a new generation of wheeled military vehicles, but a lack of money and foresight meant that these plans were slow to come to fruition. Many of the World War II vehicles were to remain in service for a further 25 years.

During the war, Canada had produced what might be considered hybrid vehicles that embraced US automotive technology and design practice, but tended to attempt to follow British War Office specifications. Although many of these CMP vehicles remained in service in Canada, and for that matter in Australia, after the end of the war obsolescence was imminent. Not long after 1945, this policy was abandoned when the Canadian Government elected to supply their armed forces with US equipment.

In Germany, many military vehicles were destroyed while others were overhauled for civilian use. New German-built trucks were frequently supplied to the Allied occupying powers. It was not until 1956 that the newly formed *Bundeswehr* was allowed to start purchasing military vehicles.

The US Army continued to use vehicles of World War II origin during the immediate post-war years – vehicles such as the Jeep, the GMC CCKW and the Dodge WC series remained a common sight, serving in Korea, Berlin, Japan and anywhere that US troops were deployed. New designs began to appear in the early 1950s and the opportunity was taken to rationalize

ABOVE: **Many trucks were left in scrapyards across Europe. This is a rare US-built Federal 605 or 606 tractor, originally equipped as a wrecker.**

the weight classes and types of vehicle produced. The 1½-ton 4x4 class was abandoned and new 5-ton 6x6 trucks replaced the mixture of 4-, 6- and 7½-ton vehicles that remained from the war years. A similar 10-ton 6x6 chassis was also subsequently produced. These post-war US trucks were produced by more than one manufacturer to the same design and were widely exported. Many remained in service to the end of the century.

BELOW: **All across Europe, companies offered surplus military vehicles that had been converted to better suit a civilian usage. This Canadian-built Dodge T110 has been converted to a timber tractor by Sworder Motors in Britain.**

The US Military Assistance Program (MAP)

In 1947, during one of the coldest winters of the century, US General George C. Marshall returned from a fact-finding mission. He was shocked by conditions in the shattered and starving countries of Europe. Marshall told President Truman that all of Europe could fall to Communism unless steps were taken to stimulate the ailing economies. Despite a counter-proposal from Treasury Secretary Henry Morgenthau who suggested that Germany should be made to pay massive reparations, Truman agreed with Marshall. On July 12, 1947, the Marshall Aid Plan was unveiled to a meeting of the 16 participating European nations. Congress voted for $13 billion in aid, the major beneficiaries of which were Britain and France. Although invited, Stalin saw the plan as a plot to undermine the Soviet Union, and he vetoed participation by any of the Soviet satellite countries.

The enabling legislation was passed on April 3, 1948, and the first ships, containing 19,000 tons of wheat, set sail from Texas to France. The Plan also saw Europe receive supplies of fuel, raw materials, goods and food. There were also loans of money and expertise to rebuild shattered factories. For four years (1948–52) US aid flowed into Europe, stimulating rapid economic growth and halting the spread of Communism.

As part of this same strategy of containing Communism, the USA had already pledged an initial $650 million in foreign aid as part of a plan to promote economic development, create political stability and build military strength among US allies. The aid was generally extended to countries bordering the Soviet Bloc as well as to those located in strategic areas such as South Asia and

ABOVE LEFT: **Convoy of Marshall Aid Plan trucks bringing Ford agricultural tractors to the Netherlands.** ABOVE: **The US post-war M Series 6x6 trucks were widely used during the Vietnam War. Many were supplied to the Army of the Republic of Vietnam, seen here withdrawing from Cambodia in 1989.**

the Middle East. Key beneficiaries included South Korea, the Philippines and Iran, but aid also went to Latin America to support pro-United States regimes.

In October 1949, Truman went further and a "Military Assistance Program" was created as a key part of the "Mutual Defense Assistance Act". The Act promised assistance to any US ally that might be threatened by the Soviet Union or one of its allies. Aid and assistance would be suspended to nations that traded in strategic materials and technologies with the Soviet Union. The initial budget was $1.3 billion but, during the first three years, military aid was supplied to the nations of Western Europe, including military vehicles to the value of $8 billion.

By 1951, the "Mutual Security Act" had replaced the Marshall Aid Plan, and economic and military aid was being offered to Europe and across the developing world. During the first year alone, European nations received military aid amounting to $1.02 billion. A year later Taiwan and Indochina received $202 million in military support. Between 1949 and 1952, less than one third of the $28 billion in aid parcelled out by the Marshall Plan had been for military use. In the following eight years, military aid grew to 50 per cent of the $43 billion in total. Aid was used to promote a free market that was seen as being beneficial to the US.

LEFT: **The Philippines was among the recipients of US aid. Here, combat-ready Philippine troops head to the front in a US-built M Series 6x6 truck. The wire mesh grille is typical of late production but the "MAP" versions of these trucks lacked various features of the US Army versions.**

With regard to military vehicles, the recipients of US "MAP" aid were given access to budget or austerity versions of standard vehicles of the period, including a restricted range of armoured fighting vehicles. This not only brought the money back into the US defence industry but also helped to spread US military influence around the world. For example, there were militarized versions of the Jeep CJ3B, designated M606; a simplified version of the M38A1 under the designation CJ5M (M606A1 etc), a simplified MAP version of the M715 designated AM715; and low-cost versions of the 2½-ton and 5-ton 6x6 trucks. All of these were supplied to Vietnam, the Philippines and other friendly nations. In some cases, the vehicles were assembled under licence in the country concerned.

Critics levelled the accusation that US military assistance promoted corrupt government, funded the imperial ventures of France and the Netherlands in South-east Asia and established the basis for modern multi-national corporations. While these accusations may or may not have been true, the plans did do little to hurt American interests around the globe.

LEFT: **Built between 1964 and 1968, the M606 was a militarized version of the standard Kaiser-Jeep CJ3B model and was intended for recipients of "MAP" aid. A licence-built version was also produced by Mitsubishi in Japan.**

The British post-war military vehicle programme

For the British Army, the multiplicity of vehicle types used during World War II had been a salutary reminder of the dangers of poor planning. A War Office Policy Committee document produced in September 1944 stated that there were close to 600 different makes and types of soft-skin transport (described as Category B) vehicles in service. Many of these were based on commercial types not suited to the needs of a modern mechanized army. A large number had been assembled by companies with no British production facility, so servicing and maintaining this diverse fleet was a huge problem.

Anxious to avoid future repetition, even before the war was over, the War Office and the Ministry of Supply had approached the Society of Motor Manufacturers & Traders (SMMT) for assistance in planning new standardized vehicles. However, a rigidly held view in War Office departments was that military-vehicle design had become widely divergent from mainstream commercial vehicles. Thus there was a curious reluctance to ask the motor industry to simply get on with the job. This view led to the notion that all Category B vehicles should be originated by the Government's design and research body – at the time, the Fighting Vehicle Design Department (FVDD). By June 1947, this principle had been agreed upon and protected by a General Staff Policy Statement, but it soon became clear that the country could not afford such luxury. By 1950, it was

ABOVE: **With some 11,500 examples built, the FV1801 Austin "Champ" was the most numerous of the British post-war "combat" vehicles. It was intended as a replacement for the Jeep and was fitted with a torsion-bar independent suspension and a five-speed gearbox which provided all gears in both directions.**

being suggested that British military vehicles should be divided into three categories – Combat (abbreviated to CT), General Service (GS) and Commercial (CL).

The combat vehicles were described as being "specialized military vehicles with multi-wheel drive, manufactured from components not used for commercial purposes and required to give the best possible cross-country performance". Five weight classes were defined – $\frac{1}{4}$, 1, 3, 10 and 30 tons, together with a 60-ton tank transporter. Much of the design

RIGHT: **The Humber FV1600 series 1-ton truck was produced in cargo and communications variants. The vehicle was the basis for the "Pig" armoured trucks and personnel carrier.** BELOW: **Rated at 3 tons, the Vauxhall FV1300, a 6x4 tractor that never entered production.**

LEFT AND BELOW: **The FV1100 series 10-ton Leyland Martian was powered by the eight-cylinder version of the Rolls-Royce B Series engine and was the largest of the "combat" trucks. Drive to the front wheels was by revolving kingpins the same as on the wartime Mack. The rear bogie was a walking-beam design as used on the Scammell. Standard variants included a cargo truck, recovery vehicle (left) and heavy artillery tractor (below). Like the Austin and the Humber, it was also offered to the civilian market with a different engine, but the price and mechanical complexity restricted sales.**

work for these machines would be carried out at what eventually became the Fighting Vehicles Research & Development Establishment (FVRDE). The smaller vehicles were fitted with independent suspension and unconventional transmission arrangements and, aside from the two larger weight categories, the vehicles were to be powered by a Rolls-Royce B Series engine. This engine was produced in four-, six- and eight-cylinder versions, with a high percentage of component commonality. Experience gained during the D-Day landings also required the vehicles to deep-wade with a minimum of preparation.

General-service vehicles were described as being "modified versions of standard civilian vehicles, for example down-rated commercial trucks with the addition of all-wheel drive, heavy-duty wheels and tyres and standardized electrical equipment". The commercial vehicles, in the third category, were simply standard-production trucks.

All of the vehicles were described by "FV" numbers: four-figure numbers were used for vehicles in the Combat category, five-figure numbers for General Service vehicles and six-figure numbers for Commercial Vehicles. The numbers were assigned in series to each vehicle type, with a different final digit used for each variant produced. For example, the FV1600 series covered the Humber 1-ton CT family; FV16000 was used to describe the Austin K9WD, which was the equivalent 1-ton GS vehicle. FV160000 would have been assigned to the 1-ton CL range had there been one.

Endless lists of vehicles and classes were produced as the War Office and the Army wrestled with the logistics of the scheme. Weight categories were changed and dropped and, at one time, it was suggested that the CT vehicles be abandoned altogether as being too costly and complex.

By 1955, the Army had spent £150 million, with just three types of vehicle produced in quantity. First of these was the FV1800 Austin Champ, a 1/4-ton 4x4, which had been intended to replace the Jeep, but which was superseded by the cheaper and more reliable FV18000 Land Rover. The FV1600 Humber 1-ton 4x4 was a superb vehicle, but was generally surplus to requirements. Finally, there was the FV1100 Leyland 10-ton 6x6 chassis, which was eventually produced as a cargo vehicle, artillery tractor and recovery vehicle.

While all of this had been happening, there had been a growing awareness that the GS vehicles had been far more successful than had originally been envisaged. In 1956, those CT vehicles which had been produced were downgraded to GS and the War Office proposed that future British military vehicles might be better designed by the motor industry and that FVRDE's role should be one of trial and assessment.

And broadly, that was the end. Future British military vehicles shared electrical equipment and minor components, but little else. The dream of a unified range of specialized types was lost.

The US post-war programme

At the end of World War II the US Government cancelled almost all of the outstanding contracts for military vehicles, and for the next five years or so the Army continued to use those that had been produced during the war years. However, this did not stop the development of new designs and, around 1950, the first of these new, so-called "M Series", vehicles started to enter service.

Occasionally described as the "Korean War vehicles" to differentiate them from the vehicles used during World War II, these were effectively improved versions of the best of the wartime trucks. Major improvements included the use of radio-screened 24V electrical equipment and built-in basic waterproofing. More importantly, having learned the lessons of standardization during World War II, these prototype trucks were produced under development contracts that provided for the design parent company to work in conjunction with the newly formed Ordnance Tank-Automotive Center (OTAC). As a result, the trucks could not be considered to be standard commercial products and the development and manufacturing processes were contracted separately, with the intention of making it easy for more than one manufacturer to assemble any given vehicle type.

At the same time, the number of types of vehicle in service was reduced by around half, with the future fleet standardized in five weight classes – $1/4$- and $3/4$-ton trucks using a 4x4 drive line, and $2^1/2$-, 5- and 10-ton trucks with 6x6 configuration drive.

First to enter service was the $3/4$-ton 4x4 M37 which was produced by Dodge as a replacement for that company's WC series, and the $2^1/2$-ton M35 6x6, which was an improved

ABOVE: **The post-war M Series 6x6 trucks were produced in 2½-, 5- and 10-ton versions, to a very similar design. The 2½- and 5-ton versions are difficult to distinguish between. An M51 5-ton dumper truck variant leaves a landing craft.**

version of the iconic "Jimmy" of the war years. The M35 was not the only $2^1/2$-ton truck produced at this time and it was eventually superseded by the Reo-designed M44 series. As well as being manufactured by Reo, and often described as such regardless

RIGHT: **New 2½-ton M Series 6x6 trucks being prepared for shipment. Note how the US Army continued to use open cabs into the post-war years.**

The Ford-designed M151 MUTT (Military Utility Tactical Truck) was the first attempt by the US Army to improve on the Jeep of World War II. Unfortunately, despite two attempts (M151A1 and M151A2) at redesigning the suspension, the combination of a high centre of gravity and swing axles led to instability when cornering. Nevertheless, thousands were produced. The directional indicators show that the first and third vehicles in the line are the M151A1 variant.

of origin, it was also produced by Studebaker, Kaiser-Jeep, Curtiss-Wright, White and AM-General. It was a very successful design and was produced in a very large number of variants, including a tractor truck. Early versions were petrol-powered, but subsequent upgrades saw the truck fitted with diesel and multi-fuel engines.

From 1950 on, the World War II-type Jeep was replaced by the broadly similar M38 – also known as the Willys MC – and, in 1952, by the more powerful M38A1 (Willys MD). However, in 1951, the Ford Motor Company was awarded a contract to develop an entirely new Jeep-type vehicle. Although the resulting M151 "Military Utility Tactical Truck" (MUTT) was eventually built in very large numbers from 1960 by Ford, Willys, Kaiser-Jeep and AM-General, handling problems meant that it was never entirely successful.

Introduced in 1950, the 5-ton M39 6x6 trucks were very similar in design and appearance to the 2¹/₂-ton model, and were intended to replace the 4-, 6- and 7¹/₂-ton 6x6 trucks of the war years. Production was undertaken by Kaiser-Jeep, Diamond T, AM-General and International Harvester, and the trucks were powered by either a petrol, diesel or multi-fuel engine according to the date of production.

The 10-ton M123 series was introduced in 1953, and was produced by Mack and Consolidated Diesel Electric (Condec), the latter using Mack axles and transmissions. All of the 10-ton trucks used a LeRoi multi-fuel or diesel engine.

Many of this first generation of US post-war military vehicles remained in service with the US Army until the end of the century. These vehicles were also being supplied to other nations across the world, often as part of the Military Assistance Program (MAP).

The GMC CCKW was the US Army's standard logistics truck during World War II, with more than half a million produced. The CCKW remained in service into the 1950s and many were used during the Korean War. This photograph, taken in July 1950, shows British infantry being transported from Taegu up to the battlefront.

Soviet technology

ABOVE: **Introduced in 1967, the 3$\frac{1}{2}$-ton 6x6 ZiL-131 became the "workhorse" of the Soviet Army and was produced in a wide range of variants, including this anti-aircraft missile carrier.**

Until the 1930s, the Soviet Union had no domestic automotive industry, and even during the Great Patriotic War – as the Soviets termed World War II – it had little spare production capacity for transport vehicles. Domestic truck production during the war years amounted to fewer than 350,000 vehicles, but large numbers of military vehicles were supplied to the Soviets from both the USA and Britain, almost half a million coming from the USA alone.

During the period 1944–45, the Soviet authorities started work on the first generation of post-war military vehicles, but designs tended to follow the pattern of existing American vehicles. For example, the 1$\frac{1}{2}$-ton GAZ-63A 4x4, and the 2$\frac{1}{2}$-ton ZiL-157 6x6, both became the mainstay of the Red Army during the immediate post-war years. These clearly leaned heavily on the design of the Studebaker US6 trucks, some 100,000 of which had been supplied

under the Lend-Lease program during the war years. Similarly, the ZiL-485 amphibian closely resembled the GMC DUKW and the GAZ-46 was little more than an enlarged Ford GPW amphibian. Even the GAZ/UAZ-69 field car was similar to the American Jeep.

During the late 1950s, these vehicles started to be replaced by a second generation of trucks, with many of the older vehicles being passed on to the Warsaw Pact nations which formed the Soviet Union's first line of defence. The Soviet automotive industry grew rapidly in the years following World War II with major truck-manufacturing plants established, under State control, in Bryansk (BAZ), Gorkiy (GAZ), Kremenchug (KrAZ), Minsk (MAZ), Ul'yanovsk (UAZ) and Likhachev (ZiL). By 1967, the Soviet Union was one of the largest producers of trucks in the world.

RIGHT: **Developed from the 6x6 trucks supplied to the Soviet Union under the Lend-Lease Program during World War II, the ZiL-157 entered production in 1958 to replace the earlier ZiL-151. This is a licence-built version, built in China. The vehicle is here in service with the Cambodian Army in 1983.**

ABOVE: **Rated at 4¹/₂ tons, the Ural 375 series was introduced in 1961. This vehicle has been equipped as a "Stalin's Organ" multiple rocket launcher.**

By this time, a third generation of military vehicles had been introduced, many of which were also produced in civilian form. While these may still have some traces of American influence, they would certainly not have been considered sophisticated by the standards of the West, but like many Soviet products of the time they were sturdy, straightforward and reliable. Most importantly, the vehicles were available in large numbers and were capable of being operated reliably in the freezing depths of the Russian winter. The most numerous of this new generation was probably the ZiL-131, a 3¹/₂-ton 6x6 truck which was powered by a 6,000cc six-cylinder engine. Produced in large numbers and adapted for a wide variety of roles, the ZiL-131 was supplied to all the armies of the Warsaw Pact.

The Soviets also produced a number of large 8x8 chassis which were designed to be used as "Transporter-Erector-Launcher" (TEL) vehicles for the growing range of surface-launched missiles. These were either trailer-mounted or carried on launch rails attached directly to the chassis of the truck. One of these, the ZiL-135L4 was powered by two large capacity V8 petrol engines, each arranged to drive the wheels on one side of the vehicle through hydro-mechanical transmission. Again, the emphasis was on the use of simple or well-proven technology which could be relied upon to produce uncomplicated vehicles in large numbers. While the Soviets might not have been able to win the technology race, if a war did occur it is probable that they could have overwhelmed the Western forces by sheer numbers.

In recent years, the break-up of the former Soviet Union has either resulted in the collapse of the former State-owned enterprises or, as in the case of Minsk Tractor (the former MAZ plant), has encouraged companies to look for overseas markets. Soviet technology remains uncomplicated to Western eyes, but it is becoming increasingly common to see Soviet trucks that have been improved by the use of an American or German diesel engine and transmission.

LEFT: **Dating from 1978, the 4-ton Ural-4320 was a diesel-engined development of the Ural-375D.** BELOW: **The GAZ-66 4x4 truck dates from 1963 and was widely used by the Soviet Army. A version was available for the civilian market.**

The Jeep effect

The Jeep of World War II was an extraordinary vehicle. Although nothing like it had really existed before, its designers worked against the clock, lacking sufficient time to reason through the inevitable design problems and the lack of any extended development period. It could be argued that it was actually rather too small but, at the same time, it quickly proved to be both reliable and durable. More than 635,000 were produced. Jeeps were used by all of the Allies and the vehicle was adapted to a wide range of roles, both in support and

ABOVE: The Soviet Union received large numbers of US-built Jeeps during World War II and produced their own version, the GAZ-67, during the war. In 1956, this was replaced by the GAZ/UAZ-69 (above) which was constructed both as a light truck and as a five-seater field car.

combat. Thousands of Jeeps remained in service after the end of the war and large numbers were allocated to the newly liberated European nations.

In the US, the original MB/GPW was replaced by the very similar M38 and then by the heavier and more powerful M38A1. The US Marine Corps purchased the lightweight "Mighty Mite" which was designed by members of the same

ABOVE: In 1948, the prototype for the Land Rover was actually built on the chassis of a military surplus Jeep. RIGHT: Built by Willys-Overland from 1954, the M606A2 and A3 Jeeps were militarized versions of the CJ5 intended for the "MAP" programme. This M606 has been restored and painted in Israeli Defense Force finish.

LEFT: **In the mid-1950s, Auto-Union DKW produced the MUNGA field car for the** *Bundeswehr* **(West German Army). It was an unusual design featuring a three-cylinder two-stroke engine and independent suspension using transverse leaf springs. The components of the front and rear axles were interchangeable. Production continued until 1968. The vehicle was also supplied to the Dutch Army.**

team that had been responsible for the original Bantam BRC40 in 1940. During the early 1950s, Ford started the design work on the M151 which, despite being produced in large numbers, suffered from handling problems. After 25 years of service, the M151 was replaced by the High-Mobility Multi-purpose Wheeled Vehicle that is generally described by the acronym "HMMWV".

The "HMMWV" effectively ended the career of the Jeep in US military service, but it appears that every country who received supplies of Jeeps believed that they could produce a better version. Many tried but failed!

The War Office intended that the FV1800 Austin Champ would be the replacement for the Jeep in British service but with its independent suspension, 5F5R transmission and Rolls-Royce engine, the design was complex and expensive. The vehicle was so unreliable that within 10 years of its introduction it had been replaced by the cheaper and simpler Land Rover. Although not originally intended as a military vehicle, it is well known that the Land Rover design had been inspired by the Jeep. The prototype used a war-surplus Jeep chassis.

Like the British, the French military authorities believed that they could design and produce a Jeep-type vehicle as a replacement for the original. The Delahaye VLR-D that was introduced in 1950 suffered transmission, handling and reliability problems so severe that it was superseded by a licence-built Hotchkiss version of the original Jeep. The French-built Hotchkiss M201 remained in service with the French Army until the end of the 20th century.

In 1955, the newly liberated West German *Bundeswehr* chose the curious Auto-Union MUNGA, independently sprung three-cylinder engined vehicle, over similar types produced by Porsche and Goliath. Following an abortive Franco-German-Italian amphibious field car designed by Hotchkiss, Büssing-NAG and Lancia, the MUNGA was replaced by the VW Iltis,

ABOVE: **In Japan, Mitsubishi produced a version of the CJ3B Jeep. Designated CJ3B-J4, production began in 1953, with large numbers supplied to the Japanese Self Defence Force, South Korea and South Vietnam. A number were also supplied to the US forces in Japan and to the domestic market. An ambulance variant was also available.**

a vehicle which perhaps owed more to the original VW *Typ* 82 *Kübelwagen* of 1939 than the Jeep.

Both Alfa-Romeo and Fiat built small Jeep-like vehicles at the beginning of the 1950s, the 1900M *Matta* (Crazy) and the AR59 Campagnola respectively. Both featured independent front suspension. Similarities with the original Jeep were there and both would have been very familiar to the men who had designed it 10 years earlier. In the Soviet Union, GAZ and later UAZ, produced small four-wheel-drive field cars which owed more than a modest debt to the original Jeep. Similar vehicles appeared in other countries as far apart as Czechoslovakia, India, Turkey and Japan.

In the near-70 years which have elapsed since American Bantam produced the first Jeep prototype, the type has become both a legend and an icon. The Jeep is probably the most recognizable vehicle in the world. An unnamed American advertising copywriter probably got it exactly right when he wrote "The sun never sets on the Willys Jeep" in 1942.

RIGHT: **The US Army's "M Series" 6x6 was produced by Diamond T, International, Mack, Kaiser-Jeep and AM-General for more than 30 years. The original power unit was a Continental petrol engine, but this was later superseded by a multi-fuel diesel.**

NATO and US influence

Formed in 1949, the North Atlantic Treaty Organization (NATO, or OTAN in French) is an alliance of 26 countries from Europe and North America dedicated to upholding the principles of the North Atlantic Treaty, specifically with regard to uniting their efforts "for collective defence and for the preservation of peace and security". The Treaty was signed in Washington, DC on April 4, 1949, and the signatories included the five Treaty of Brussels states (Belgium, France, Luxembourg, the Netherlands and the United Kingdom), as

well as the United States, Canada, Portugal, Italy, Norway, Denmark and Iceland. Three years later, on February 18, 1952, Greece and Turkey also joined. In 1954, the Soviet Union suggested that it should join NATO to preserve peace in Europe. The proposal was rejected by the NATO countries, who suspected the Soviet Union's motives.

When West Germany was incorporated into the organization on May 9, 1955, the Soviet Union responded by creating the Warsaw Pact, thereby defining the two opposing sides of the "Cold War". The Warsaw Pact was signed on May 14, 1955, by the Soviet Union, Hungary, Czechoslovakia, Poland, Bulgaria, Romania, Albania and East Germany. In 1966, France withdrew from the military membership of NATO.

For the first few years, NATO was not much more than a political association and even during the height of the "Cold War", NATO did not participate in any actual military engagement as an organization. However, the Treaty provided for mutual defence in the face of an armed attack on any member, and it became apparent that a military role for NATO was unavoidable. During the Korean War member states agreed to the development of an integrated military structure, which was built-up under the direction of two US Supreme Commanders. This has brought about considerable standardization of military terminology, procedures and technology among the NATO countries, although in practice it has meant that the European countries have largely adopted US military practice. Standardization is controlled by the publication of so-called Standardization Agreements – known

ABOVE: **Rated at 10 tons, the British-built AEC Militant was used with the Leyland Hippo as part of the UK's force in NATO.**

LEFT: **Post-war DAF military vehicles were part-financed by US aid and for this reason were fitted with Hercules engines. This is the 3-ton YA314 dating from 1955.**

as STANAGs – by the NATO Standardization Agency in Brussels. They are written in English and French, the two official languages of NATO. Something like 1,300 STANAGs have been published covering an enormous variety of military land, sea and air related topics. Vehicle-related standardization has covered road signs, sizes and capacities of vehicle batteries, inter-vehicle starting sockets, towing hitches, vehicle marking, bridge classifications, trailer connectors, load markings and many other topics.

In 1955–56, NATO laid down standardization requirements for vehicles in load classes of $^1/_4$, 1, 3, 6 and 10 tons. Despite a number of US-German and Franco-German initiatives,

efforts aimed at producing a series of standard military vehicles in each class, for use by all member countries, have failed. In the main, however, member nations have produced vehicles which fall into the standard weight classes and which have been designed under the relevant STANAG agreements – with the notable exception of the USA. For some unaccountable reason they have decided to retain $^1/_4$-, 1-, $2^1/_2$-, 5- and 10-ton class vehicles.

It is unlikely that NATO would ever be able to agree on a standard vehicle range, but these standards have at least ensured a high level of commonality and interchangeability.

LEFT: **The British Humber FV1600 was a 1-ton 4x4 truck produced in cargo and radio variants. It was a sophisticated vehicle, powered by a Rolls-Royce petrol engine. This vehicle is fitted with torsion-bar independent suspension on all four wheels.**

Warsaw Pact military vehicles

The Soviet-sponsored "Treaty of Friendship, Co-operation and Mutual Assistance" – more generally known as the Warsaw Pact – was signed on May 14, 1955, at the Presidential Palace in Warsaw, Poland. In the West it was seen as a direct response to West Germany joining the North Atlantic Treaty Organization (NATO) in 1955. It was, effectively, the Communist Bloc's counterpart to NATO and was a military-treaty organization of Communist states in central and eastern Europe. The founding members were Albania, Bulgaria, Czechoslovakia, Hungary, Poland, Romania and the Soviet Union. The Soviet Union cited the Warsaw Pact when crushing the Hungarian Revolution in 1956, while Albania withdrew from the Treaty in September 1968 in protest against the Soviet invasion of Czechoslovakia. This was never recognized by the Soviet Union.

ABOVE LEFT: **Dating from 1962, the East German-built (GDR) P3 was a seven-seat field car, powered by a 2,407cc six-cylinder engine. Independent torsion-bar suspension and differential locks at front and rear.** ABOVE: **Also produced in East Germany, the IFA W50LA/A was introduced in 1969 and was equipped for a variety of roles. This is a public-address van intended for internal security service.**

The Warsaw Pact was divided into two branches – the Political Consultative Committee, which co-ordinated non-military activities, and the Unified Command of Pact Armed Forces, which had authority over the troops assigned to it by member states. The latter was headed by a Supreme Commander, who was also the First Deputy Minister of Defence of the USSR.

Since 1945, the Soviet Union had been acting as the arsenal of Eastern Europe, and the Warsaw Pact simply ensured that

RIGHT: **The Soviet ZiL-157 was widely used by all of the Soviet Bloc nations and was also produced under licence in China. Standard variants included the cargo/ personnel truck (shown), tractor, shop van, multiple rocket launcher, tanker, snow plough and bridging vehicle. Like many Red Army vehicles, it was fitted with a Central Tyre Inflation System (CTIS).**

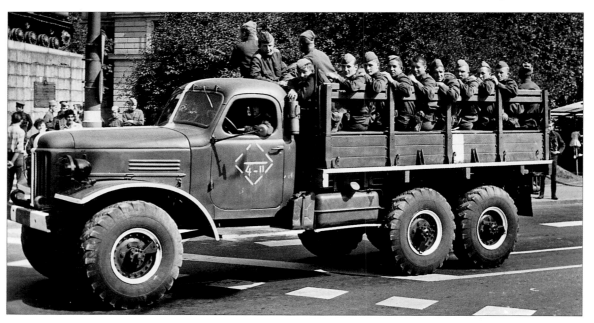

this situation would continue. The signatory nations were "encouraged" to buy Soviet military equipment, including uniforms and all kinds of vehicles, or were allowed to build vehicles and other equipment under licence. For example, the Polish Lublin-51 was effectively the GAZ-51 while the UMMM M-461 produced in Romania was similar to the Soviet GAZ/UAZ-69. This not only helped the Soviet economy, but also resulted in the standardization of military equipment across the Pact states. However, some of the vehicles supplied were effectively obsolete types superseded by the introduction of new designs in the Soviet Union.

Beginning in the late 1960s, the Soviet Union conducted a dramatic increase in the mechanization of their ground combat forces, but the technology remained resolutely outdated. Soviet military vehicles, for example, were robust and easy to operate. When new vehicles were introduced they were fitted wherever possible, with equipment and proven sub-assemblies and components already in use.

The Soviet Union was never able to achieve total standardization among the member states of the Warsaw Pact. The nationalized and state-run motor industries of Poland, Czechoslovakia, Hungary, East Germany and Romania produced military trucks, motorcycles and armoured vehicles for use by their own forces. There was also considerable trading among the member states. For example, trucks produced by Robur in East Germany and Tatra in Czechoslovakia were exported to Romania and Poland.

In 1973, the Warsaw Pact nations were able to call upon a regular army of more than three million men, plus a further three million reservists; these were equipped with more than 78,900 tanks. More than 10,000 surface-to-air missiles were ranged along what most considered to be the European border. Papers released since the demise of the Warsaw Pact have revealed that, until the 1980s, military plans in the case of war

ABOVE: **A late model of the East German-built Robur LO-1800A truck. The Robur factory was based in Zittau until 1961 and continued production of the Phänomen Granit. Production then turned to the LO-1800A.**

with the West were for a swift land offensive, the objective of which would be to secure Western Europe quickly. There was no ban on the use of nuclear weapons and Poland alone was home to 178 nuclear missiles, increasing to 250 in the late 1980s. Warsaw Pact commanders made very few plans for the possibility of fighting a defensive war on Soviet territory.

The end came with the fall of the Berlin Wall in 1989 and the subsequent political collapse of the Soviet Union. On March 12, 1999, the former Warsaw Pact members and successor states Hungary, Poland and the Czech Republic joined NATO. Bulgaria, Estonia, Latvia, Lithuania, Romania and Slovakia joined in March 2004.

LEFT: **A ZiL-151 mounted** *Katyusha* **rocket launcher being used to attack an apartment building, photographed in Lebanon in 1975. The vehicle is one of thousands supplied to Syria by the Soviet Government. The 6x6 ZiL-151 was produced from 1947 until 1958 when it was replaced by the ZiL-157.**

RIGHT: **To fit a Jeep into a glider, in this case an Airspeed AS.51 Horsa, it was necessary to cut back the ends of the front bumpers, remove the steps behind the front mudguards, and provide some means of easily and quickly removing the steering wheel. Only then could the vehicle be turned at the top of the ramp and fitted under the main wing spar which ran across the inside of the fuselage.**

Air-portable vehicles

The concept of air portability for vehicles dates back to World War II when motorcycles, light trucks and, eventually, light tanks were delivered by glider. The size of the transport aircraft of the period meant that, at first, it was necessary to adapt existing vehicles for this purpose. For example, in 1943, Nuffield Mechanizations shortened and otherwise heavily modified a Willys Jeep for possible delivery by air. In the USA, Willys, as well as Crossly Chevrolet and Kaiser, also produced lightweight versions of the Jeep.

Improvements in the load-carrying capabilities of transport aircraft and gliders finally rendered these experiments unnecessary. During the Normandy and Arnhem operations, modified Jeeps were carried in Waco Hadrian and Airspeed Horsa gliders. Experiments were also conducted on dropping a Jeep on an airborne platform or "crate" slung underneath, for

example, a Handley Page Halifax. The British Ministry of Supply ordered 2,000 such platforms for airborne operations in 1944.

Throughout World War II one of the major constraints affecting delivery by air of all types of load, not only vehicles, was the size and shape of the aircraft cargo door and the volume of the fuselage. By the late 1950s, aircraft such as the Blackburn Beverley, with a huge rear loading door, removed this constraint and paved the way for the development of new equipment.

In Britain, heavy dropping equipment (the delivery of vehicles by parachute) included the AATDC (Army Air Transport and Development Centre) platform, which had capacity for a Jeep and trailer or 3,636kg/8,000lb of stores, the 8,181kg/18,000lb Medium Stressed Platform (MSP), and the Heavy Stressed Platform (HSP) which was suitable for air-dropping a bulldozer for example. Similarly, a vehicle

RIGHT: **Air-portable (APD) variant of the Bedford QLD GS truck, shown here with the upper part of the cab and doors removed to reduce the overall height. The top of the cab is stowed in the rear body. Once the truck had been stripped, the chassis was mounted on castors and was carried in one Dakota, while the body parts and the wheels were carried in a second aircraft.**

ABOVE: **Austin "Champ" loaded on to the Medium Stressed Platform (MSP) ready for air-dropping.** LEFT: **US "HMMWV" slung beneath a Chinook heavy-lift helicopter in Afghanistan. Although perfectly practical, and often the only feasible method of moving vehicles across hostile territory, this is an expensive solution.**

could be slung under a helicopter; the Royal Marines deployed Citroën 2CV pick-ups in this way.

Similar equipment was developed in other countries. The US Army, for example, used a system of modular platforms to rig vehicles for air-dropping. Adjustable diagonal braces were used to secure the load to the platform and thick honeycomb packing was employed as a shock absorber.

Over the years, the increasing size and capability of transport aircraft began to make the weight of individual vehicles in drops less relevant. However, this did not prevent many armies from developing vehicles specifically designed to

maximize the dimensions and capabilities of transport aircraft. In Britain, one of these was the Land Rover "Air Portable General Purpose" (APGP), an amphibious vehicle dating from the early 1960s designed to be stacked two-high inside an aircraft fuselage or dropped on the medium stressed platform. In 1964, a specification was issued for a lightweight version of the Land Rover that could be stripped to the minimum for air-portability, while remaining fully operational. It was intended that this vehicle would be carried by the Beverley, Argosy and Belfast aircraft which made up the RAF heavy airlift fleet at the time. The vehicle could also be under-slung beneath a Belvedere or Wessex helicopter.

Other specialized vehicles began to appear which were sufficiently small and versatile to allow easy delivery by air. Examples include the Belgian FN AS24, which weighed just 220kg/485lb and yet could carry four lightly equipped troops. In France, the LOHR FL500 was developed for use by airborne troops, with six vehicles carried in a C-130 Hercules or C-160 Transall aircraft. The M274 "Mechanical Mule" was a similar vehicle produced for the US Army. The German Kraka 640 folding lightweight vehicle was even more versatile, and 16 folded or 10 unfolded vehicles could be carried in a C-160. Similarly, the EINSA MM-1 multi-purpose all-terrain vehicle from Spain is sufficiently small to allow ten to be carried in a C-130.

Common standards and procedures have been developed by NATO to simplify the air delivery of all kinds of supplies. In Britain, for example, the co-ordinating body is the Joint Air Delivery Test & Evaluation Unit (JADTEU). The US-built Lockheed Martin C-130 remains the standard military transport aircraft in the West and can carry a range of loads, including utility helicopters and six-wheeled armoured vehicles. In an air-delivery role, loads up to 19,090kg/42,000lb can be dropped.

ABOVE: **An air-portable and amphibious 8x8 vehicle of the Chinese Peoples' Liberation Army.**

79

Reconnaissance and special operations vehicles

The development of the Jeep effectively created a new class of military vehicle. With a powerful four-cylinder engine and excellent four-wheel drive, the Jeep could go almost anywhere. The Special Air Services Regiment (SAS) in Britain soon adapted the vehicle for special behind-the-lines operations. The vehicles were stripped to the bare essentials, loaded with food rations, water, personal kit and jerrycans of fuel. SAS Jeeps were able to carry everything, including machine-guns, the crews needed to conduct interdiction raids on enemy airfields, and fuel and ammunition dumps.

In the early 1950s, with the Jeeps beginning to wear out, the SAS adapted the short-wheelbase Series I Land Rover for the same role. In Belgium, the Para-Commandos similarly converted the Minerva TT to this role, carrying out a series of similar

modifications. The SAS Series I remained in service until the late-1960s when it was replaced by the long-wheelbase Series IIA which provided more stowage space and allowed the operating range to be increased.

The military requirements for what was officially known as "Truck, GS, SAS, 3/4-ton, 4x4, Rover 11" – but which everyone refers to as the "Pink Panther" – were drawn up by the SAS Regiment in 1964 and derived from experience gained on operations. Some improvised prototypes were produced in conjunction with the Royal Electrical & Mechanical Engineers (REME) workshop, but it was clear that the standard Series II chassis was not suitable. Final development of the vehicle was passed to the Fighting Vehicles Research & Development Establishment (FVRDE) who produced a development vehicle based on a long-wheelbase Series II equipped with heavy-duty springs and over-sized wheels fitting 9.00–15 sand tyres.

LEFT: **A beautifully restored Land Rover Series I as used by the British Special Air Service.**

ABOVE: **Built by Marshalls of Cambridge, and dating from the late-1980s, the SAS special patrol vehicle finally replaced the iconic "Pink Panther".**
RIGHT: **Constructed by Marshalls of Cambridge, the iconic Series IIA-based "Pink Panther" is typical of long-range patrol vehicles, carrying weapons, stores, spare parts, fuel and whatever is needed to allow the crew to survive behind enemy lines for days at a time.**

Other changes included the use of two long-range fuel tanks, which increased the average operating range to 2,500km/ 1,500 miles, and the inclusion of various weapons mounts.

By May 1967, a final specification had been prepared and Marshalls of Cambridge was contracted to develop the vehicle, and build 72 examples. The first, by now using the Series IIA chassis, was ready in August 1968. Following some inevitable detail changes, the SAS received the first vehicle on October 2, 1968.

Following stalwart service, the "Pink Panthers" started to be replaced in the late 1980s by a heavily modified Defender 110 "Desert Patrol Vehicle" (DPV). Superficially resembling the "Pink Panther", the DPV lacked doors, windscreen, top and frame. At the rear, the body was of the civilian high-capacity pick-up truck. An external roll-over bar was fitted behind the front seats. Also there were additional fuel tanks, as well as generous stowage capacity for additional petrol and water jerrycans, ammo and personal kit. A pair of machine-guns was mounted in the rear, with a third pedestal-mounted on the scuttle.

In 1992, Land Rover introduced the "Special Operations Vehicle" (SOV), based on the long-wheelbase four-door Defender 110, featuring a combined roll bar and weapons mount. The SOV was originally designed to provide the US Army Rangers with a rapid-reaction, air-portable, all-terrain weapons platform. Believing that the ubiquitous High-Mobility Multi-purpose Wheeled Vehicle (HMMWV) was too large, the Rangers had been impressed by the performance of the British Army's Defenders during the first Iraq War, seeing it as a better replacement for the M151A2 gun Jeep. The Rangers took delivery of 60 examples in 1993, and the SOV was also offered to other defence customers.

A year later, Land Rover showed the "Multi-Role Combat Vehicle" (MRCV) at the British Army Equipment Exhibition (BAEE). Developed partly in conjunction with Longline, who had produced the "desert buggies" favoured by the SAS, the MRCV was also derived from the Defender and was originally demonstrated on the short-wheelbase Defender 90, but users could also choose the Defender 110 or 130 platform. The MRCV was subsequently renamed the "Rapid Deployment Vehicle" (RDV).

The RDV was intended to provide maximum versatility, acting either as a weapons platform or reconnaissance vehicle. The modular construction enabled the vehicle to be converted for seven distinct roles. These included pedestal mount, MILAN anti-tank platform, multi-purpose ring mount, and personnel or cargo carrier. Conversion from one role to another required only hand tools, and no modifications were required which would have compromised the vehicle's ability to be used for general service duties. The RDV could also accept the "Weapons Mount Installation Kit" (WMIK), which was developed for use with the British Army's Wolf Defender XD 110 models.

Like the original SAS Jeeps, these special operations vehicles are designed to get special forces in and out of an area fast and have given rise to a whole new sub-category of military vehicle – the soft-skin combat vehicle. It is a category in which the Land Rover has a unique position.

ABOVE: **The distinctive brush guard identifies this special operations vehicle developed for the US Rangers following "Operation Desert Storm", the first Gulf War.**

RIGHT: **Leyland-Scammell "Medium Mobility Load Carrier" (MMLC) DROPS vehicle. Note how the load-carrying area can be used to transport a light armoured fighting vehicle such as the Scorpion.**

Cargo vehicles and DROPS

The cargo vehicle, or simple load carrier, forms the basis of military logistics and provided the first steps towards the mechanization of most armies. Almost all of the early motorized military vehicles were assigned to the cargo-carrying role, and by the end of World War I most mechanized armies had divided load carriers into three categories – light, medium and heavy – covering payloads of up to 1 ton, $1^{1}/_{2}$–4 tons, and over 5 tons respectively. By the mid-1930s, trucks were also being categorized as those that were suitable only for road use, and those equipped with all-wheel drive to enhance off-road performance.

While the development of trucks continued rapidly after the end of World War I, there were no particular advances in those designed for a logistical role. The cargo carriers of the 1920s and 1930s were generally rigid chassis four- or six-wheeled trucks, often with fixed sides that meant loading had to be done from the rear. Tractor and trailer units were not much

ABOVE: **Although these are standard cargo trucks, the US Army's Oshkosh 8x8 "Heavy Expanded Mobility Tactical Truck" (HEMTT) was also fitted with the "Palletized Loading System" (PLS). The trucks are being unloaded prior to deployment in "Operation Desert Storm", the first Gulf War.**

favoured, even during World War II, although, at least by the end of the war, the upper limit for the heavy class vehicles had risen to 10 tons. The story was no different during the post-war years. Trucks became larger, more powerful and more reliable, but remained little different in concept from vehicles of 50 years earlier. From the late 1960s it started to become common practice to fit larger trucks with hydraulic cranes for loading and unloading – these were described by the British Army as "Crane Appliance, Lorry Mounted" (CALM).

The biggest, and really the only technological improvement in load carrying, came in the 1980s with the use of self-loading "Demountable Rack Off-loading and Pick-up System" (DROPS) vehicles designed to handle flat-racks.

Work on DROPS had begun in the 1970s when it became obvious that the British Government would not be prepared to fund the numbers of logistical vehicles required to keep battle supplies flowing to the combat units in the event of war. Clearly a more radical approach was required to the problems of supply. Commercial transport companies had been using demountable bodies for some time and, at the end of the 1970s, the Royal Corps of Transport (now the Royal Logistics Corps) undertook feasibility studies into the adaptation of this system for military use. In July 1982, the Ministry of Defence requested submissions from vehicle and load-handling system manufacturers for trials. A year later, Foden Lorries and the Scammell Trucks Division of Leyland were asked to produce "Medium Mobility Load Carriers" (MMLC) and "Improved Medium Mobility Load Carriers" (IMMLC) incorporating DROPS equipment for evaluation.

The DROPS system is made up of a removable vehicle container body and flat-rack pallets, manufactured to the ISO (International Standards Organization) standard dimensions. These flat-racks, which carry 10 NATO pallets to a total weight of 15 tons, are designed to be carried by vehicles equipped with special mechanical load-handling systems. The equipment allows the container or flat-rack to be picked up from the ground

ABOVE: **The Foden "Improved Medium Mobility Load Carrier" (IMMLC) DROPS vehicle incorporated the same equipment as the Scammell. The Foden proved to have better cross-country performance.**

ABOVE: **Foden 10-ton 6x6 cargo truck fitted with a hydraulic lifting arm to facilitate the loading and unloading of cargo – the British Army describe this as a "Crane Appliance, Lorry Mounted" (CALM).**

and loaded over the rear axles on to the chassis of the transporter vehicle without any need for manual handling or breaking down of the load. This means that the load can be moved from stores to end user, across a variety of vehicles if necessary, without ever needing to be unpacked. Indeed, the flat-racks and containers can be easily transferred from road to rail and back again with no need for conventional mechanical-handling equipment. The system can be operated by one man, and the speed of loading means that the DROPS system provides increased efficiency.

The military version of this bulk transportation system, which is described by the US Army as the "Palletized Loading System" (PLS), includes features which are not required by civilian users, including below-ground pick-up, high tolerance to mis-alignment of the LHS and flat-rack, and the ability to travel across country without compromizing the security of the load.

Since the initial deliveries and deployment of the British Army's DROPS system began in early 1990, the range of body options has been expanded to include, for example, vehicle-handling pallets, communications shelters, tankers, hospital modules, workshops and radar installations.

Similar load-handling systems are also in use with most armies in the West, using standard ISO-dimensioned flat-racks

ABOVE: **Although it was subsequently re-rated at 4-tons, the 3-ton Bedford RL 4x4 is a typical type of military cargo vehicle since the early days of World War II. Most such vehicles can also be used as troop carriers.**

and container bodies. In the USA, for example, Oshkosh fits an OTC/Multilift LHS on the 10-ton M1120 8x8 "Heavy Expanded Mobility Tactical Truck" (HEMTT) chassis. In Germany, Multilift load-handling equipment has been installed on MAN chassis. In France, the Renault TRM 10,000 6x6 is equipped with the Bennes-Marrel load-handling system. Users include Astra, Volvo, Scania, Sisu, Steyr and others.

LEFT: **Although most commonly specified as a basic cargo vehicle, the French-built ACMAT is a versatile vehicle which can be readily adapted for a variety of roles including gun tractor, personnel carrier, mortar carrier, shelter carrier and water tanker. The vehicle shown is in service with the French Foreign Legion during UN operations.**

RIGHT: **This 1-ton forward-control Land Rover was fitted with a four-stretcher Marshalls body for use as an ambulance for forward areas. The red cross markings are applied to hinged flaps which can be closed to show just the camouflaged green finish. A similar type of ambulance was produced for the Luxembourg Army.**

Ambulances and medical vehicles

Motorized ambulances were among the first types of military vehicle to be developed, with all of the major combatants of World War I using small van-type ambulances, and motorcycle combinations also used as stretcher carriers. Most offered very little in the way of comfort for the casualty and many injured soldiers must have perished as a result of the jolting ride across country, never actually reaching sanctuary. The development of bodies for military ambulances continued during the inter-war period, with Germany and Britain both producing standard designs that could be fitted to a number of chassis.

ABOVE: **The current British Army forward area ambulance is based on a Land Rover Wolf Defender XD long-wheelbase chassis.**

During World War II, if there was nothing else available, the Allied armies favoured the use of the Jeep for front-line evacuation. There were three standard designs employed, one of which placed the stretchers above the driver, the other two placing the wounded men in a lower, less precarious position, either behind the driver or across the bonnet.

The British Army's standard heavy ambulance of World War II was based on the Austin K2Y chassis and provided accommodation for four stretchers or ten seated casualties in an enclosed and heated body. The US equivalent was the Dodge WC54, which could also accommodate four stretchers or eight seated in a somewhat smaller body, but with the benefit of four-wheel drive. Both types were supplied to other Allied armies. Germany and the USA also used standard bus bodies in the ambulance medical role behind the lines. The standard *Wehrmacht* front-line ambulance (*Krankenwagen*) body of World War II was designated Kfz 31, and could be fitted to a number of light 4x2, 4x4 and 6x4 chassis.

By the time the war was over, armoured ambulances had begun to be used, the best of these being a vehicle based on the Canadian-built C15TA armoured truck. Others were based on the White M3A1 scout car or the International half-track. The *Wehrmacht* also used the half-tracked Hanomag SdKfz 251/8 as a front-line armoured ambulance.

The requirements of the medical evacuation role have changed little since World War II, and front-line military ambulances have continued to be produced on 4x4 type chassis. The standards of care available to casualties during evacuation to a clearing station or hospital have been much improved.

ABOVE: **A field ambulance based on the Renault R2087 4x4 chassis which was used in service by the French Army during the 1950s.**

ABOVE: **With go-anywhere performance, the Jeep was adapted to serve as a front-line ambulance, although it must have been far from comfortable.**

In the USA, there have been field ambulances built on the M38A1 and M151 chassis, and the current US front-line ambulance is based on the ubiquitous AM-General "High-Mobility Multi-purpose Wheeled Vehicle" (HMMWV). The British Land Rover Series I and the Austin "Champ" were both fitted with stretcher kits in the early 1950s, rather in the style of the wartime Jeep. Later, the long-wheelbase Land Rover was adopted for the standard British field ambulance, and mountain crash rescue vehicle in the mid-1950s. The current British vehicle of this type uses the 3,327mm/130in variant of the Land Rover Defender chassis.

Medium and heavy ambulances have tended to be built on a suitable truck chassis, often with softer suspension to minimize discomfort. For example, in Britain there have been larger ambulances based on the Ford Thames E3, Austin K9 and Bedford RL chassis. There were also armoured ambulance variants of the Alvis Saracen, FV430 series and Humber "Pig". In France, Peugeot and Renault medium truck chassis have been used, while in the USA, the 3/4-ton Dodge and 1-ton Kaiser-Jeep chassis have both been fitted with ambulance bodies.

Other military medical vehicles produced over the years include mountain search and rescue vehicles, mobile operating theatres, dental surgeries, medical laboratories, X-ray units and medical supply vehicles. These included various refrigerated vehicles for the delivery of blood and plasma.

LEFT: **A *Bundeswehr* armoured battlefield ambulance built on a Bucher/MOWAG 6x6 DURO chassis. The vehicle has more space for stowage of medical equipment and supplies and also additional personnel accommodation. The larger, boxy body enables the medical teams to provide more than basic first-aid treatment to battlefield casualties.**

RIGHT: **A Jeep, equipped for signals equipment cable laying, in Normandy, 1944, with a GMC truck in the background.**

Communications vehicles

Marconi made his history-making cross-Channel radio transmission in 1898. It was obvious that wireless would have military applications, and a British Royal Engineer Committee, headed by Captain J. C. Kennedy, was set up the following year to keep a watching brief on his progress. By 1901, Marconi had proposed a mobile wireless station for military use, the heavy equipment being mounted on a Thornycroft steam-powered wagon. Within five years, the Royal Engineer Signal Service had accepted wireless as a standard means of communication, and mobile equipment was mounted in Daimler and Rolls-Royce motor vehicles, as well as in horse-drawn wagons.

Alongside more traditional messaging systems, which included the use of pigeons and motorcycle despatch riders, both sides used telegraph and telephone transmissions for messages during World War I, as well as establishing wireless stations in the trenches and behind the lines. Mobile wireless equipment was also carried in motor vehicles, fitted with a telescopic mast-type or folding aerial made of steel tubing which could be quickly raised or lowered.

In 1920, the British Army established the Royal Corps of Signals and during the 1920s and 1930s there was considerable development in both cable and wireless

communication. Gradually, Morse code began to be replaced, or at least supplemented, by voice communication. Command tanks were among vehicles to be fitted with wireless equipment.

By the time World War II broke out, radio sets – although the British persisted in calling them "wireless" – had been reduced in size sufficiently to allow installation in vehicles as small as a Jeep or staff car. It became common practice with both the Allies and the Axis armies to equip most, though not all, armoured cars and tanks with a radio set that would allow communication both with headquarters and between individual vehicles. The *Wehrmacht* pioneered the use of unit construction, with interconnection between radio sets made by plug and socket. Multi-channel "Frequency Modulation" (FM) sets began to be developed which provided front-line troops with reliable, static-free communications. These were followed by "Very-High Frequency" (VHF) and "Ultra-High Frequency" (UHF) sets which increased range and reliability, particularly where line-of-sight transmission was not possible. Specialized communications vehicles, often with a self-contained generating capability, were used by both sides during the war.

Equipment became smaller, more powerful and considerably more sophisticated during the 1950s and 1960s. The development of printed-circuit technology

and transistors allowed a degree of miniaturization that was further exploited when the integrated circuit appeared. Another breakthrough came in December 1958 when the US Signal Corps launched its first communications satellite, "Project Score", demonstrating the feasibility of world-wide communications by means of relatively simple active-satellite relays. During the Vietnam War, the US Army utilized "troposcatter" technology, whereby a radio signal is beamed up into the atmosphere and bounced back down to earth, by-passing challenging terrain which might interfere with more conventional communications.

In 1988, the US Signal Corps embarked on the production and deployment of the "Mobile-Subscriber Equipment" system (MSE) which effectively created a dedicated mobile telephone network serving the battlefield. This allowed a commander or communications centre to connect mobile telephones and fax machines in vehicles with each other, sending and receiving secure information. It even allowed connection to the public telephone network. The MSE was mounted in "High-Mobility Multi-purpose Wheeled Vehicles" (HMMWVs), rather than the larger, less-mobile 2½-ton 6x6 trucks.

By the 1990s, new military communications technology allowed signals to be transmitted across many frequencies, hopping from one to another at high speed. This allowed many channels of talk to share an already crowded frequency spectrum. Later generations of these radios combined encryption devices with the receiver/transmitter, making it possible to send and receive digital traffic with great fidelity.

Alongside the advances in voice and signals communications, there have been similar technological improvements in electronics devoted to target acquisition, surveillance and intelligence gathering, fire-control and digital data processing. While the specialized vehicles that were used for voice communications may be a thing of the past, the modern army continues to deploy formidable electronic resources, much of it mobile and vehicle-mounted.

ABOVE: **The Land Rover Vampire, a signals-equipped variant built on the forward-control 101 chassis. It is also thought to have been used as a re-broadcast or relay vehicle.**

ABOVE: **Bedford QL fitted with mobile teleprinter equipment.** BELOW: **The Bedford QLR was equipped with a house-type body for signals, command and similar roles. The electrical system was interference suppressed, and equipment included a 600W auxiliary generator.**

Heavy equipment transporters

As World War II progressed, the size and weight of tanks deployed by the opposing armies increased inexorably. The massive German *Königstiger* (King Tiger), which appeared in 1944, weighed some 70 tons, and the Germans had even larger tanks on the drawing board. After the end of the war, there was no relief and the trend increased. Post-war tanks such as the British Conqueror and the Soviet *Iosif Stalin* (Joseph Stalin) still weighed more than 60 tons. Most current "Main Battle Tanks" (MBTs) tend to weigh around 65–70 tons. The challenge has been to produce tank transporters – or "Heavy Equipment Transporters" (HETs) – to move these enormous vehicles.

During the war years, the Allies had three tank transporters available – the Diamond T Model 980/981 ballasted tractor, which was used with a 40–45-ton multi-wheeled draw-bar

ABOVE: **The British-built Scammell Commander replaced the Thornycroft Antar in 1982. In 2001, the Commander was replaced by the Oshkosh M1070F.**

trailer; the Pacific TR-1 – better known as the M26 "Dragon Wagon" – which was available in both soft-skin and armoured form, and designed to be coupled to a Fruehauf 40-ton semi-trailer; and the Scammell Pioneer, which was used only by Britain, and which was also designed for use with a semi-trailer. In Germany and the Soviet Union, it was common practice to move tanks on their tracks or on railway wagons. The heavy purpose-designed transporters favoured by Britain and the US Army did not exist.

Having never been rated as "standard", the Diamond T was quickly phased out by the US Army, who continued to use the

RIGHT: **In the early 1970s, Germany and the USA agreed to co-operate in the development of a new main battle tank, the MBT-70. It was also agreed that there would be a jointly developed heavy equipment transporter, the HET-70, to carry the new tank. The HET-70 project was eventually abandoned but each country continued with the development of the HET. The US-designed vehicle was the Chrysler XM745.**

"Dragon Wagon". However, both the Pacific and the Diamond T remained in service in Britain and Europe into the early post-war years. Britain even chose to re-engine the aging, but very capable, Diamond T, keeping some examples in reserve service into the 1970s.

The US Army experimented with a number of tractor and trailer combinations during the 1950s and 1960s, including a double-ended twin-tractor outfit designed at Detroit Arsenal towards the end of the 1950s. In the 1960s, there were further experiments with a 10x4 heavy tractor coupled to a semi-trailer. Although the development of the joint US-German MBT-70 main battle tank was cancelled, the associated transporter evolved into the Chrysler XM745 8x8 tractor and the German Faun SLT-50 *Elefant*. In US service, the Chrysler was replaced by the 50-ton Oshkosh M911 6x6 in 1976 and then, when the M1A1 Abrams MBT started to enter service in 1992, by the Oshkosh M1070 tank with a 70-ton semi-trailer.

In Britain, attempts were made to produce specialized 30- and 60-ton tractors, but when these were abandoned, the Diamond Ts were supplemented by the Thornycroft Antar. Initially rated at 50 tons and designed for use with a draw-bar trailer, it was subsequently upgraded to 60 tons and produced both as a ballasted tractor and for use with a semi-trailer. Although the Rotinoff Super Atlantic was trialled in the late 1950s, the Ministry of Defence (MoD) retained the Antar until 1982 when it was replaced by the 65-ton Scammell Commander. By the time the Commander was due for replacement, in the 1990s, the European Union had imposed a 12-ton axle loading limit which forced a rethink. In 2001, the MoD announced that it had chosen a European version of the US-built Oshkosh M1070, with a seven-axle 72-ton King trailer, in preference to the Alvis-Unipower MH 8875.

By the late 1950s, the heavy equipment transporter had standardized its present design configuration; essentially a powerful diesel-engined tractor, not necessarily with all-wheel drive, coupled to a multi-axle semi-trailer. A winch is usually fitted behind the cab to aid the loading of disabled tanks. As well as those described, similar tractors have been produced in France by Renault, Willème, Berliet and Saviem, in Germany by Magirus, Mercedes-Benz and Faun, in Spain by Fiat. Other types have been produced in Sweden, China, South Africa, Belarus and elsewhere.

The Soviet Army still prefers to move tanks on their tracks, but the 8x8 MAZ-537 tractor has been used as a heavy equipment transporter in conjunction with a low-loader semi-trailer.

ABOVE: **The Thornycroft Antar was originally designed as a private venture for oil-field use but was adopted by the British Army as a replacement for the Diamond T Model 980/981. This is the Antar Mk 3, fitted with a ballast body.**

Missile transporters

Although dating back several centuries, the military rocket began to find new favour in the mid-1930s. Its reappearance coincided with the development of solventless cordite which could be shaped into a solid propellant. The use of liquid propellants allowed the Germans to develop long-range rockets as a substitute for artillery, a method also used by the Soviet Union. During World War II, the *Wehrmacht* and Soviet armies both employed mobile rocket launchers, mounting electrically operated multiple tube launchers on to trucks and half-tracks. The modern form of this weapon is the US-built "Multiple Launch Rocket System" (MLRS) carried on a tracked chassis.

The German V2 was the first modern ground-launched missile, but, lacking a guidance system, it was really only useful as a terror weapon. Although the V2 gave rise to similar rockets in both the USA and the Soviet Union, it was not considered to be transportable.

The US Army's "Honest John" missile of the early 1950s was probably the first transportable surface-launched artillery missile, although it still lacked a guidance system. It was widely deployed by NATO armies and saw service in the USA, Canada, Britain, Japan and West Germany during the 1950s and 1960s. Designed to deliver either a conventional or nuclear warhead, the missile was carried on a special "Transporter-Erector-Launcher" (TEL) which was mounted on the chassis of a standard US Army 5-ton 6x6 truck. Reload missiles were carried in open-backed trucks and on special trailers.

The "Honest John" had actually been preceded by the Firestone "Corporal" guided-weapon system, which was derived from the German V2 rocket, but the system was large and complex and required specially designed launch and transport vehicles, as well as erector vehicles, servicing platforms, fuel dispensers, and firing systems. A similar surface-to-surface missile system was produced in Britain under the designation "Blue Water". Although it never entered service (the project being

TOP: **Soviet ZiL-131 tractors towing semi-trailers for transporting surface-to-air missiles during a May Day parade.** ABOVE: **The US Army's "Honest John" missile was also deployed by Britain, West Germany, Canada and Japan.**

ABOVE: **US Army "Tube-launched, Optically guided, Wire-tracked" (TOW) battlefield anti-tank missile launched from a "HMMWV" vehicle.**

cancelled in August 1962) "Blue Water" was sufficiently compact to allow transport and launch from a 3-ton Bedford RL.

The "Corporal", "Honest John" and its replacement, "Sergeant", were eventually superseded by the "Lance" missile which was carried on a tracked chassis derived from the US Army's M113 armoured personnel carrier.

LEFT: **A "Javelin" anti-tank missile being fired from a Pinzgauer vehicle of 42 Commando, Royal Marines, during a live fire demonstration.**

During the two or three decades following the end of World War II, the Soviet Union developed a range of huge "Transporter-Erector-Launcher (TEL) vehicles to handle the nuclear and conventional ballistic missiles deployed by the Red Army. The first of these were the V2-based mobile missiles, mounted on a railway launcher, which were developed during the late-1940s. Truck-mounted launchers began to be used by the mid to late-1950s. The most notable of Soviet rocket was probably the MAZ-543 truck-mounted SCUD which saw service with Iraqi forces during the Gulf War of 1992. The Soviet Union continued to develop transportable ground-launched ballistic missiles long after the concept had fallen from favour in the West, where the military tended to favour submarine launch or aircraft delivery. The longest-range Soviet ballistic missile of this type was the Temp-S, SS-12 (NATO codename: "Scaleboard"), which had a range of 900km/550 miles. It was in service between 1965 and 1979 and was carried on a MAZ-543 truck.

The equivalent US missile systems include the M48 "Chaparral", which is carried on a tracked chassis, and the "Patriot", which is mounted on a wheeled "Transporter-Erector-Launcher" (TEL) vehicle and requires support vehicles carrying radar and data-processing equipment.

For battlefield use, there has been a trend towards the miniaturization of both anti-tank and anti-aircraft guided weapons and associated equipment. British surface-to-air anti-aircraft missiles like the "Thunderbird" of the 1960s could be carried on a small trailer and towed by a Bedford 3-ton truck, or even a Land Rover. Surface-to-air anti-aircraft missile systems such as the "Rapier" can be trailer-mounted and towed behind a Land Rover or mounted in the back of a tracked launcher vehicle. As regards anti-tank missiles, even first-generation weapons such as the "Malkara", "Vigilant" and "Swingfire" were sufficiently compact that the launch system and guidance equipment could be carried in a small armoured vehicle such as a "Ferret" or "Saladin". Current practice is to mount modern anti-tank weapons, such as the wire-guided Franco-German MILAN system or the US-built TOW and "Dragon" missiles, on to small soft-skin vehicles such as the "HMMWV", Land Rover or Jeep.

LEFT: **Soviet MAZ-543 9P120 "Transporter-Erector-Launcher" (TEL) loaded with a Temp SS-12b missile (NATO name: "Scaleboard"). The missile is contained inside a protective cylinder which, until ready for launch, allows the fuel for the solid-fuel rocket motors to remain at a controlled temperature.**

Bridging vehicles

ABOVE: **The US Army "Mobile Assault Bridge" (MAB) dates from 1959.**
Each 4x4 transporter vehicle carries either an end bay or an interior bay.

Despite the development of heavy-lift helicopters, surface crossing of water obstacles continues to play a vital role in the capability of the modern army. As early as 1812, the British Army had used floating pontoons to provide a simple ferry. Tank bridges began to be developed during World War I. Smaller types of portable bridge, which were carried by specially adapted trucks, began to appear in the 1930s. During this period, the British Army, for example, used several types of bridge, including the prefabricated floating pontoon, trestle, small box-girder bridge and sliding bay bridge; all were designed to be carried on a 3-ton 6x4 truck.

In 1941, the British-developed "Bailey" bridge system was adopted by the Allied armies as the standard military bridging system, providing a versatile means of quickly building a range of bridges from prefabricated standardized girder components. Part of the design criteria was that the individual components could be carried by a six-man party, and the parts had to be transportable in a 3-ton truck. The system was used extensively throughout the European campaign and was also produced in the USA, with a total of

490,000 tons of bridge components manufactured, sufficient to build a 40km/25-mile long bridge. One example, the "Springbok" bridge, which was constructed over the River Po at Pontelagasco in Italy, used 1,900 tons of equipment. In 1942, the "Bailey" suspension bridge was introduced, designed for clear spans of up to 122m/400ft. In modified form, the "Bailey" bridge remains in use to this day.

During World War II, the US Army also used the H10 and H20 box-girder bridges, a steel pontoon bridge and two types of floating pontoon bridge. Once again, all of these were carried on specially adapted trucks. The *Wehrmacht* used pneumatic boats to assemble light bridges. Some of their engineer units were equipped with box-girder bridges, while permanent river crossings were built using the *Typ B* (pontoon trestle), *Typ K* (box-girder), *Typ J* (tank bridge) or *Typ LZ* (through-girder bridge).

Floating pontoon and girder bridges are the mainstay of military bridging equipment, as are the mechanized "Armoured Vehicle Launched Bridges" (AVLBs) mounted on what are essentially modified tank chassis. More recently, floating

RIGHT: **The Gillois-EWK bridge and ferry system was a joint Franco-German project, at first using rubber floats. Subsequently these were replaced by fabricated aluminium buoyancy units. The system of a separate ramp and bridging units can be used to assemble either a floating bridge or a motorized ferry.**

ABOVE: **Folding float unit carried on a US Army Oshkosh (HEMTT) truck.**
LEFT: **Royal Engineers assembling elements of the British Army's "Bridging in the 90s" (BR90) system (see caption below).**

bridge and ferry systems have been developed which allow speedy crossing of water obstacles.

NATO strategy of the 1950s and 1960s had decreed that repelling a Soviet invasion across the plains of East German would require considerable amphibious capability. While this might have been all very well for small numbers of tactical vehicles, it was impractical for the larger numbers of supply vehicles that are required to keep an army fighting. The question of providing mechanized bridges occupied much military thinking, and various kinds of floating and folding bridges were developed by both NATO and the Warsaw Pact.

Floating bridges were not a new idea, the US Army having already deployed such devices during World War II. What was new was the idea of using vehicles equipped for transporting and erecting the bridge, remaining a part of it while it was being used. One of the earliest of these was a unique amphibious bridging and ferrying system designed in the early 1950s by a French General, Jean Gillois. The first example in this development programme was the Gillois-EWK bridge and ferry system, "an amphibious vehicle, which can be used as a water-crossing ferry or can be assembled with other such vehicles to form a pontoon bridge… (it includes) a hull section hinged to two ramp sections". Essentially, the system is made up of separate ramp and bridge vehicles that were used to build either a Class 60 floating bridge or a navigable ferry. Both types of vehicle were equipped with huge inflatable rubber pontoons, supported on curved frames and carried on rigid arms hinged on the sides of the hull. Some 264 of these vehicles were produced before the design was superseded by the improved M2, on which the easily damaged rubber floats were replaced by rigid aluminium buoyancy units which folded up and on to the hull for transport.

At the same time, the US Army also developed a similar bridging vehicle which was described as the "Mobile Assault Bridge" (MAB).

LEFT: **The BR90 system is a beam-launched bridge which can be assembled on one side of a river crossing and levered across. This photograph was taken during trials.**

Amphibious vehicles

During the 1950s and 1960s, NATO placed considerable emphasis on the development of amphibious vehicles. It was believed that a Soviet invasion would cross the East German plains and that the Soviets would have destroyed as many river crossings as possible. Serious experiments were conducted with a view to making vehicles of all sizes capable of floating or deep-water wading, and various amphibious vehicles were produced as a result. Most armies were able to field small armoured vehicles which were amphibious or capable of being made amphibious. Russia remains an enthusiastic user of the amphibious combat vehicle.

Wartime amphibious vehicles included the US-built DUKW, which was based on the GMC 6x6 truck, the Jeep-based Ford GPW, and the Porsche-designed VW *Schwimmwagen*. The DUKW can almost certainly be considered the most successful amphibious military vehicle of all time and, unsurprisingly, provided the model for many of the vehicles which followed. Other less successful vehicles were produced by Britain and Japan.

In the USA, GMC produced prototypes for the so-called "Super Duck" around 1953, with a 2$\frac{1}{2}$- to 4-ton cargo capacity. In 1956, this was followed by the 8x8 "Drake" with an increased payload of 8–10 tons. Both were amphibious trucks which were equally suited (or equally unsuitable) on roads or relatively calm water. The LARC (Lighter, Amphibious, Resupply, Cargo) and BARC (Barge, Amphibious, Resupply, Cargo) were more like boats that were also fitted with wheels, enabling them to traverse beaches or loading ramps. There is no question that these vehicles could have been used in road-going supply convoys. Other US trucks which were required to provide some degree of amphibious operation included the M561 "Gama Goat" and the Caterpillar "Goer" family. Also the 5-ton 8x8 cargo vehicle prototyped in 1959–60 by Ford and others, such as the "Mover". It would be better to consider these as trucks which could float, should it be necessary, rather than fully amphibious vehicles.

The DUKW remained in service with the British Army for many years after the war, but it was eventually superseded by the Alvis Stalwart, a 5-ton 6x6 high-mobility load carrier

ABOVE: **The 5-ton Alvis Stalwart used Dowty Hydrojet units driven from the main engine for both propulsion and directional control in the water.** RIGHT: **Prototyped in 1962–63, the US Army's Ford XM656 amphibious 8x8 truck was fitted with inflatable seals on the cab and body doors.**

LEFT: **The DUKW was extremely useful in ferrying supplies from ship to shore in many amphibious assaults during World War II.** BELOW: **While it is no longer thought there is any specific need for amphibious logistics vehicles, most military trucks, like this Finnish-built Sisu, are expected to be driven ashore from landing craft.**

that was fully amphibious. Unlike the US-built DUKW, and the "Super Duck" and "Drake" experiments, the Stalwart was both steered and powered in the water by a Dowty Hydrojet system that provided improved performance. Notwithstanding drive-line problems caused by having just one differential, the Stalwart remained in service for 25–30 years. For the last 10 years in service the truck lacked any amphibious capability since the Hydrojet system was removed. There were also experiments with amphibious Land Rovers, both in Britain and Australia.

Berliet almost negotiated a licence to manufacture the Stalwart under the name Aurochs, but declined at the last minute. Marmon-Bocquet produced a similar 4-ton 4x4 amphibious truck which used Dowty Hydrojets for propulsion in the water. France, Germany and Italy also co-operated on the early development stages of an amphibious Jeep-type vehicle that would have been manufactured by Hotchkiss, Büssing and Lancia, but the project never passed the prototype stage.

The Soviet Union had used large numbers of Ford GPW amphibians during World War II and built a virtual copy, the GAZ-46 in the post-war years. Similarly, a DUKW copy was built from 1952 as the ZiL-485. Dating from the end of the 1950s, the LuAZ-967M was a small amphibious vehicle intended for ferrying supplies to the front line across difficult terrain, or for evacuating casualties carried on stretchers either side of the central driving position.

The truth is that the performance requirements for the two modes of operation of an amphibious vehicle are in conflict and most such vehicles are neither good trucks nor good boats. By the end of the century it was widely accepted that heavy-lift helicopters could be used to fulfil the role previously allocated to amphibious trucks, and such vehicles that remained in service were consigned to ferrying supplies from ship to shore.

ABOVE: **Britain's attempt at building a domestic rival to the DUKW was the eight-wheeled skid-steered Morris-Commercial Terrapin of which 500 examples were built. Designed by Thornycroft, the vehicle was powered by two Ford V8 petrol engines, each driving the four wheels along one side of the vehicle. The lack of suspension made it difficult to drive on the road.**

Index

AKNOWLEDGEMENTS

Picture research for this book
was carried out by Pat Ware
and Jasper Spencer-Smith, who
have selected images from the
following sources: JSS Collection,
Warehouse Publications, Getty
Images, Tank Museum, Imperial
War Museum, Archives of Canada
and Ullstein Bild. Much of the
colour material has been
supplied by the following
(l=left, r=right, t=top, b=bottom,
m=middle):
John Blackman: 27b; 40t; 44br;
49tr; 49b; 52b; 80m; 95t.
Paul Costen: 81tr.
Phil Royal: 38–9; 41m, 41b; 53b;
80t; 80b; 81tl; 81b; 87t.
Simon Thomson: 1; 2; 3; 4; 5;
45t; 46t; 47t; 47bl; 47br; 48t;
48bl; 50b; 52t; 53tl; 60b; 72t;
72br; 73t; 74t; 74b; 75t; 75b; 76tl;
76tr; 77t; 81tr; 84t; 84b; 87b.
Every effort has been made
to acknowledge photographs
correctly, however we apologize
for any unintentional omissions,
which will be corrected in
future editions.

LEFT: **The Jeep effectively replaced
the motorcycle in military service.**